the cake chronicles

the cake chronicles

Bake a Journey Through 60 Incredible Creations!

ana zelić
Creator of Ana's Baking Chronicles

PAGE STREET
PUBLISHING CO.

PAGE STREET
PUBLISHING CO.

First published in 2021 by

Page Street Publishing Co.

27 Congress Street, Suite 105

Salem, MA 01970

www.pagestreetpublishing.com

Distributed by Macmillan, sales in Canada by The Canadian Manda Group.

25   24   23   22   21   1   2   3   4   5

ISBN-13: 978-1-64567-381-1

ISBN-10: 1-64567-381-2

Library of Congress Control Number: 2021931339

Cover and book design by Laura Benton for Page Street Publishing Co.

Photography by Ana Zelić

Printed and bound in the United States

To all you cake-loving home bakers

Contents

Introduction

I've been actively in the kitchen since I was twelve years old, and I've always loved it.

It started with occasionally making easy lunches before school for my brother, sister and me, but since Mum was handling the cooking part pretty awesomely, I kind of leaned into baking. Having a sweet tooth might have helped, too. Actually, when I think about it now, I feel that good, delicious food was an integral part of my upbringing. Watching cooking shows and discussing food was a family activity. When I wasn't studying and bingeing on teen drama TV shows, you bet I was online searching for more *MasterChef* and *Great British Bake Off* episodes.

During my studies, I spent more and more time in the kitchen. Baking helped calm my anxiety; it was comforting, and it was my happy place. I loved creating something beautiful and delicious from just a handful of basic ingredients. The whole process of whisking, beating, kneading and being covered in flour had a very soothing effect on me, and it still does. Of course, sharing the baked goods with my loved ones and seeing their happy, satisfied faces is still one of my favorite parts of baking. The dirty dishes? Not so much.

With so much of my time focused on baking, it wasn't long before I became absolutely mesmerized by the tall, beautiful layer cakes we didn't really have in Croatia. Soon I was dreaming of having my own modern, trendy bakery but, after a brief experience of working in a pastry shop, I figured out that wasn't the route I wanted to take. I needed much more freedom and creative space, so starting a blog was actually the best thing I've done for myself so far. I dove all in, without really knowing anything about running one.

I started teaching myself all about the science behind baking even before the blog, but having one only pushed me to learn more and more. You see, I'm all about the flavor. That was the main reason I started developing my own recipes. Playing with science, reactions and percentages to get exactly what I want makes me one happy nerd and I'm tremendously happy that I get to share my work with others. With you.

Why cakes?

Well, I feel like layer cakes are the epitome of luxury, celebratory desserts. Their glorious looks leave you in awe—even if I lean toward simple, elegant design—but it's their incredible combination of flavors and textures that makes you fall in love with them. That's why in this book you'll find that more than half of the recipes are layer cakes. With soft and moist cake layers, silky frostings and luscious fillings—it's no wonder they are THE dessert for special occasions. And sometimes that special occasion involves you and your favorite TV show. Remember, there is always a reason to celebrate.

But fret not—I've also included some easy, less time-consuming bakes, such as Bundt cakes, sheet cakes and cheesecakes, so I've got you covered on even the busiest days of the week.

However, I feel I should issue a fair warning to all my American readers: In this book you will not find recipes for American buttercream or meringue-based buttercreams. You might be wondering, well . . . what's left? Plenty of delicious, less sweet frostings that put flavor first, while still being great choices for decorating, because I know we eat with our eyes first.

Baking should be fun, so if you're only starting your baking journey, allow yourself to be a beginner. Allow yourself to fail sometimes—I sure did, but always persevered. A little practice goes a long way.

For me, it all started with cakes, but there are still so many things that excite me and that I want to learn. Because, when we stop learning, what is there left to do?

I hope the recipes in this book help you create new memories, inspire you to try new things and maybe lead you to find some new favorites. Now, get your apron, put on your favorite music and get baking!

Assembling a Layer Cake

I know a lot of people, especially beginner bakers, are often intimidated by stacking magnificent, tall layer cakes. How do I know that? Well, because I've been there! From worrying whether it will collapse or the filling will ooze out, or how to cut it—let me tell you, I've been in your shoes, making mistakes every step of the way. I still do sometimes when I'm rushing things, but at least now I know the culprit.

Here I wanted to share with you a couple of hints, tips and step-by-step images of the instructions you'll find in the recipes to encourage you and help you bake your way through this book. Prepare to make a mistake or two either way, but that's okay! I'm a firm believer that it's practice that makes perfect, no matter how much theory you know.

Tip #1 My number one tip is to take two days to make a cake, if your schedule allows it. I usually prepare the buttercream base, any fillings and the cake layers the night before assembling and serving. That way, everything has enough time to chill and you're not rushed. Chilled cake layers are much easier to handle and stack, so I almost always double wrap them in plastic wrap and chill them in the fridge overnight. That way you don't have to worry about your cake drying out and you'll be more confident the next day when you're ready to stack it. You can keep cake layers refrigerated like this for a couple of days.

Tip #2 Level the cake layers. Cakes are naturally a little domed and there is nothing wrong with that, but if you're looking for really even-looking layers and more stable stacking, then I suggest you level the cakes (and enjoy the scraps as a reward for all your hard work!). Using a cake leveler is the easiest way to do this, but if you're handy you can use a long, serrated knife, too. Some people even use toothpicks and thread, but I've never personally tried this method.

Tip #3 Using a turntable and a cake board (or a serving plate or stand) that's at least 1 inch (2.5 cm) bigger than the circumference of your cake really goes a long way toward achieving that perfectly frosted cake. A plastic turntable still serves me well to this day, so don't feel that you need the most expensive one!

Tip #4 When you're applying the first layer of frosting around the cake, also known as a crumb coat, make sure not to return back to the bowl any of the scraped frosting that contains crumbs.

Tip #5 In addition to Tip #4, make sure to clean the cake scraper or the palette knife in between smoothing the cake. If there's a lot of frosting residue and it's clean, without any crumbs, return the frosting to the bowl and wipe the cake scraper clean with some paper towels before going for another try.

Tip #6 There are only so many attempts you can make at trying to smooth the frosting perfectly before you lose your mind. Been there, done that. If you don't succeed by your third try, just leave it be—the most important thing is that your cake is delicious.

Tip #7 However, if the frosting is stubborn, thick and has a lot of bubbles, give it a beat with a silicone spatula to knock the air out before frosting your cake. You can also try to heat the outside of the bowl with a hair dryer, because it's much easier to smooth out softer frosting, and it will firm up quickly on the chilled cake. On the other hand, if the frosting seems too soft, just place it in the fridge for 15 minutes to firm up.

Tip #8 Working with smaller tools is always easier because it allows you to have more control, so I recommend having a couple of small offset palette knives. They're my most used tool when it comes to making cakes.

Tip #9 When filling the cake, always make sure to leave enough frosting for the outer layers and decorations. I'm always afraid of not having enough frosting, so when following the recipes in this book, you might have some left over in the end until you've gotten a bit more practice.

Tip #10 If your curd or jam filling came out thin or you've overfilled the cake and you're afraid it will slide, stick a couple of skewers down from the top and into the middle of the cake, carefully crumb coat it and put in the fridge to set. After it has firmed up, you can take out the skewers and apply the final layer of frosting.

Step-by-Step Images

1. Start by leveling the tops of your cakes using a cake leveler or a serrated knife.

2. Evenly spread the frosting over the first cake layer using an offset palette knife.

3. Make a buttercream border around the edges to keep any filling in.

4. Carefully pour the filling inside the buttercream border.

5. Repeat this process then top with the final cake layer, placed upside down.

6. Apply a thin layer of frosting on the sides of the cake to create a crumb coat.

7. Make sure to coat the top of the cake as well.

8. Smooth the crumb coat with a cake scraper. Chill for 30 to 60 minutes.

9. Cover the whole cake with the rest of the buttercream as evenly as possible.

10. Using a cake scraper, smooth the sides of the cake.

11. Smooth the top by gently pulling the buttercream edges toward the center using an offset palette knife.

12. Ta-da! Your cake is assembled and ready for decorating.

Tips and Troubleshooting

Three golden rules for using this book:

1. All ingredients should be at room temperature prior to using so they can all emulsify smoothly, unless specifically stated otherwise.

2. All the recipes in this book were developed and tested using only metric measurements and a kitchen scale. The US cup and spoon measurements are provided for your convenience, but I highly recommend getting a digital kitchen scale and measuring in metrics. It will transform your baking experience.

3. The quality of the ingredients determines the quality and the taste of the end bake, so choose well and always go for full-fat ingredients.

Cake Pan Conversion Table

Almost all the layer cake recipes in this book are baked in three 6-inch (15-cm)-wide and 2-inch (5-cm)-tall anodized aluminum pans. The measurements listed in the recipes can also be used to make a three-layer 7-inch (18-cm) cake, a two-layer 8-inch (20-cm) cake or a four-layer 6-inch (15-cm) cake, all with slightly thinner layers than the original dimensions. Keep an eye on the baking time if you change the pan size.

Alternatively, you can easily convert the measurements to fully fill larger cake pans to create a three-layer cake by using the multiplication factors in the following table for all ingredients in the recipe.

Example 1: 3 eggs x 1.75 = 5.25 (5¼) eggs ≈ 5 eggs

Example 2: 250 g (2 cups) all-purpose flour x 1.75 = 437.5 g ≈ 440 g (3½ cups)

With such ingredients as eggs, feel free to use the nearest round number. In this case, that's five eggs for a three-layer 8-inch (20-cm) cake. If you need to measure half an egg, whisk it, weigh the whole whisked egg, then use half.

> **Note:** These calculations are great for the cake batter; however, you may end up with some leftover buttercream. I also don't recommend working with more than a double batch at once, because the ratios might be off when using a large quantity of ingredients.

Storing

Since most of the recipes have dairy-based frostings, I wouldn't let assembled cakes sit at room temperature, in an airtight container, for longer than two days. You can keep them tightly covered in plastic wrap (double, if possible) or in an airtight container in the fridge for up to a week, but allow the cake to come to room temperature before serving, so they have time to soften.

That said, the fridge will dry out your cake, so the longer the cake sits in the fridge, the drier it will get, especially if it is not properly covered.

Freezing Cakes

You can prepare the cake layers in advance, double wrap them in plastic wrap and keep them in the fridge for up to 3 days or freeze them for up to 3 months, for best results.

	7-inch (18-cm)	8-inch (20-cm)	9-inch (23-cm)	10-inch (25-cm)
Multiplication Factor	1.35	1.75	2.25	2.75
Servings	16 to 18	20 to 24	26 to 30	32 to 38

If you have leftover cake, you can freeze each slice individually, again double wrapped. Custards don't thaw well, so I would avoid freezing the cakes with a custard filling. That said, I've successfully frozen and thawed cake slices filled with ermine frosting, which is the one most used in this book, so you shouldn't have any problems.

To thaw cake layers, put them in the fridge to thaw gradually, still wrapped. This way, you'll have cold cake, which is easier to stack.

To thaw individual cake slices, place them on a plate at room temperature for about an hour, still wrapped in plastic wrap to avoid any condensation on the cake itself.

Make It Ahead

You can make all the fruit fillings, nut butters and cake layers in advance (as explained in the previous section), but for the best results, finish the buttercreams on the day of the assembly.

However, if for whatever reason you need to make the buttercream in advance, store it in an airtight container in the fridge, and when ready to use, let it come to room temperature and beat it vigorously with an electric mixer to restore the fluffiness. With butter solidifying in the fridge, the buttercream will lose some of its volume.

Please note that most of my buttercreams are made in two steps: first, mixing what I call the pudding base, which is cooked briefly and allowed to cool (and which can also be made ahead of time [see Tip #1 on page 11]), and then a later step to combine the cooled base with the butter and any additional flavorings. Please do not try to rush things by adding the remaining ingredients to the hot base.

How to Neatly Slice a Cake

Start by dividing the top of the cake into equal quarters by leaving little marks with a knife. After that, you can further divide it, depending on the size of your cake. I usually cut twelve slices, so I'll visually divide each quarter into thirds. Make sure to use a long, sharp knife. If the cake has a crunchy filling or nuts in the cake layers, use a serrated knife like a saw. Before cutting through the cake, dip the knife into hot water and lightly brush it with a paper towel. Clean the knife in the same manner before each new slice. Cakes that are slightly cold will cut more neatly, but room-temperature cakes are much more tender and delicious.

Cake Baking Troubleshooting

Sometimes things go wrong in the kitchen—it happens to all of us. Maybe you're stressed, rushed or putting too much pressure on yourself. Maybe it's just one of those days or maybe your baking powder expired. We've all been there at one point or another.

So, to help you understand what exactly went wrong and demystify possible mistakes you're making, I've narrowed down some of the most common problems that occur in cake baking and listed their culprits.

1. The cake sank in the middle.

This can happen at the beginning when you're still getting to know your oven. They're a hard nut to crack sometimes, right? This can happen for a few different reasons:

- Opening the oven door too soon will result in your cake collapsing, because the batter didn't have enough time to set and the sudden temperature change messed up the baking process.

- The cake is underbaked, so while it cools, the middle will slowly sink in.

- You used too much leavening, such as baking powder. This makes the cake rise quicker than it should and collapse while still in the oven, because there wasn't enough support to hold the rise.

2. The cake didn't rise.

Check the expiration date on your baking powder; more often than not, that's the culprit. Aside from that, there might be a lack of sufficient leavening agents or the oven temperature was too low and they weren't activated.

3. The cake is dense.

Cakes made with butter are a little bit on the dense side compared to oil-based and sponge cakes. To be honest, that's exactly why I love them. However, it is possible to make them denser (in a negative way) than they should be. Here are a few culprits:

- You didn't use room-temperature ingredients. If this is the case, the butter can't fluff up and the ingredients fail to emulsify and combine thoroughly. There is not enough aeration and you can end up with grainy and curdled batter.

- There is too much flour in the batter or the cake was overmixed after adding the flour, which resulted in more gluten development and, thus, a denser cake.

- It might sound contradictory, but too much liquid will give you a dense cake because there isn't enough support (eggs and flour) to hold the cake together.

4. The cake is dry.

Most likely the cake was overbaked or there was too much flour, possibly measured improperly if using cups instead of a scale. Try baking it a couple of minutes less next time or check whether your oven is running hot by using an oven thermometer.

5. The cake has holes in it.

This happens if the cake was overmixed or the leavening wasn't distributed in the batter properly. This doesn't necessarily mean that cake will taste bad, but it does happen sometimes.

6. The cake shrinks significantly after cooling.

Although cakes are supposed to pull away from the edges of the pan slightly, if they shrink significantly, the batter was probably overmixed and overbaked.

7. The cake stuck to the pan and/or fell apart.

This happens if the cake hasn't had time to set in the pan and is too fragile, or if it's been sitting in the pan for too long and the sugar started to crystallize. Try using a thin knife around the edges of the cake to help release it. Don't worry if you damage the cake slightly; you'll patch it up with buttercream.

8. The buttercream curdled.

The difference in temperature of the ingredients was too great. Most likely one of your ingredients was too cold; when it comes to ermine buttercream, it's either the pudding base or the butter. Not to worry; all you have to do is heat it up a little bit—I usually use a hair dryer on the outside of the bowl. Do it one bit at a time so you don't melt the butter, then keep whipping it until it comes together all fluffy and silky.

9. The buttercream is too soft.

One of two situations might have occurred:

- Your kitchen was too hot, so your ingredients were softer/hotter than needed. Place the bowl in the fridge for 20 to 30 minutes, then give it a whip with a mixer and check the consistency again.

- You tampered with the measurements and possibly added more milk or sugar, which left you with a softer pudding base and ultimately a softer buttercream.

Decadent Chocolate

Even though chocolate knows no season, I always tie it to winter. With its rich, warming flavor and its ability to come in all different shapes and sizes, I can't think of anything better to treat myself to on a cold, dark, winter day.

Since a really good chocolate bar is my preferred choice when I need to have that chocolate fix, I tend to be just slightly picky when it comes to chocolate-based desserts. But that means that you're in luck, because you can count on an excellent chocolate array in this chapter.

If you like to stay on the safe side, start with a classic combination, such as the Hazelnut Espresso Chocolate Cake (page 19) or a less time-consuming bake like the Chocolate Orange Bundt Cake (page 33).

When you're feeling incredibly chocolate deprived and you want to indulge, the Cookie Dough Brownie Cake (page 29) and Chocolate Pretzel Caramel Cake (page 37) have got your back. Make sure to share them with any chocoholics in your life—spread the love.

And if you're feeling like trying something new and exciting, don't miss the Passion Fruit Milk Chocolate Cupcakes (page 41)—you will love them.

All the recipes in this book are developed and tested using only metric measurements and a kitchen scale. The US cup and spoon measurements are provided for your convenience, but I highly recommend getting a digital kitchen scale because it will transform your baking experience.

Hazelnut Espresso **Chocolate Cake**

It seemed only fitting to start with one of my personal favorite flavor combinations. Coffee in a dessert? Count me in! Hazelnut butter brings a strong flavor to an already delicious and tender cake. As for the frosting, I chose a luscious, rich French buttercream made with egg yolks, only I used a slightly modified and easier version that is very popular in Croatia. Instead of making the hot syrup, you'll heat the eggs and sugar over a double boiler, kind of like making Swiss meringue. It's easy-peasy and doesn't require a sugar thermometer.

. . . .

Serves 12 to 14

Hazelnut Butter
5.5 oz (150 g) blanched chopped hazelnuts

1 to 2 tsp (5 to 10 ml) vegetable oil (optional)

Hazelnut Espresso Cake
Cooking spray or butter, for pans

2 cups (250 g) all-purpose flour

2 tsp (10 g) baking powder

½ tsp fine sea salt

Rounded ¾ cup (180 g) sour cream, at room temperature

2 tsp (4 g) ground instant espresso coffee (I prefer Nescafé brand)

3 tbsp (45 ml) sunflower oil

½ tsp vanilla extract

½ cup (1 stick; 115 g) unsalted butter, at room temperature

1¼ cups (250 g) granulated sugar

Rounded ⅓ cup (100 g) hazelnut butter

3 large eggs, at room temperature

Make the hazelnut butter: In a dry skillet, toast the hazelnuts over medium-high heat, stirring constantly, until golden brown and aromatic, about 3 to 4 minutes. Remove them from the heat and let cool for 10 to 15 minutes, then transfer them to a food processor and pulse until the hazelnut butter starts to look creamy and smooth. If you feel that the processing is taking too long and your food processor might be overheating, add 1 to 2 teaspoons (5 to 10 ml) of vegetable oil to help make the hazelnut butter smooth and creamy in an instant. Transfer to a clean jar and keep at room temperature until using.

Make the cake: Preheat the oven to 350°F (175°C) or 325°F (160°C) if using a fan-assisted oven. Grease three 6-inch (15-cm) round cake pans with cooking spray or butter and line the bottoms with parchment paper.

Sift the flour, baking powder and salt into a medium-sized bowl and whisk to combine. In a measuring jug, lightly whisk together the sour cream, instant coffee, sunflower oil and vanilla.

Using a stand mixer fitted with the paddle attachment, or a large bowl if using an electric hand mixer, beat the butter with half of the sugar until pale and fluffy, 2 to 3 minutes. Add the rest of the sugar along with the hazelnut butter and beat to combine. Add the eggs, one at a time, making sure each is fully incorporated before adding another.

Next, add the flour mixture in three additions, alternating with the sour cream mixture to avoid splashing and overmixing the batter. After each addition, mix the batter just until combined. Scrape the bowl a couple of times with a silicone spatula to make sure everything is mixed nicely.

Divide the batter equally by weight among the prepared pans and level it with an offset palette knife. Bake for 22 to 25 minutes. It's best to check the cakes after 22 minutes and then adjust the baking time accordingly, because ovens can vary. The cakes are done when they're springy on the top and when a skewer inserted into the middle comes out mostly clean. Remove from the oven and leave them to cool in their pans on a wire rack for 10 to 15 minutes to firm up a little bit before inverting them onto a wire rack to cool completely.

(continued)

Chocolate Espresso Buttercream

3 large egg yolks, at room temperature

2 large eggs, at room temperature

Pinch of salt

⅔ cup (130 g) granulated sugar

2 tsp (4 g) ground instant espresso coffee (I prefer Nescafé brand)

1⅛ cups (2¼ sticks; 350 g) unsalted butter, cubed and at room temperature

5.5 oz (150 g) good-quality 55% dark chocolate, melted

½ tsp vanilla extract

Make the buttercream: In a heatproof bowl, vigorously whisk together the egg yolks, eggs, salt, sugar and instant coffee until combined. Place the bowl over a pan of simmering water, making sure that it doesn't touch the water, then whisk constantly until the sugar dissolves, about 2 to 4 minutes.

Remove the bowl from the heat and beat the mixture with an electric hand mixer or stand mixer on medium-high speed for about 5 minutes, or until it is pale, doubled in volume and falls in ribbons. With the mixer still going on medium-low speed, add the butter, one cube at a time, and beat until fully incorporated. Add the melted chocolate and vanilla and beat until combined.

Assemble the cake: Start by leveling the tops of your cakes using a cake leveler or a long, serrated knife for a neater look, if needed. Then, put a little bit of buttercream in the middle of a serving plate or your cake board to keep the cake from moving around. Place it on a turntable for easier handling and decorating.

Place one cake layer on the serving plate and, using a small, offset palette knife or a piping bag filled with buttercream, spread the frosting over the top of the cake layer, about ⅜ inch (1 cm) thick. Top it with the next cake layer and repeat this process. Place the final cake layer on top, making sure it's upside down to get a nice, smooth surface on top.

Next, apply a thin layer of frosting around and on top of the cake, smoothing it with a cake scraper to keep in the crumbs. Chill the cake in the fridge for 30 to 60 minutes before applying the final coat of frosting and decorating.

Once the crumb coat is firm, frost the cake with the remaining buttercream. Smooth the sides and the top using a cake scraper and an offset palette knife. Chill the cake for 30 to 60 minutes before pouring the ganache on top.

Chocolate Ganache

2 oz (60 g) 55% dark chocolate, finely chopped

5 tbsp (75 ml) heavy cream

Meringue Kisses (page 76), for decorating (optional)

Make the chocolate ganache: Place the chocolate in a small, heatproof bowl. In a small saucepan, bring the cream to a simmer, then pour it over the chocolate. Cover with a plate and let sit for 1 to 2 minutes, or until the chocolate softens and begins to melt. Stir with a spatula until combined and smooth. Alternatively, you can do this (using a microwave-safe bowl) in a microwave in 30-second intervals. If it seems too loose, leave it to cool and thicken for 10 to 15 minutes before pouring it over the chilled cake.

When your cake is chilled and you're ready to decorate, pour two-thirds of the chocolate ganache onto the middle of your cake and slowly spread it around with a small offset palette knife for a natural-looking drip. If you need more, add the remaining third of the ganache on top and spread it in the same manner. The final quantity needed depends on how thick the ganache is and how chilled the cake is. You might end up with a little leftover ganache.

Let the chocolate ganache drip firm up in the fridge for 15 to 20 minutes and, if desired, decorate the top of the cake with meringue kisses.

Keep the cake tightly covered in plastic wrap or in an airtight container at room temperature for 2 days or in the fridge for up to a week. Allow the cake to come to room temperature before serving.

Peanut Butter Chocolate Cake

I'm one of those people who enjoys eating peanut butter straight from the jar, and I'm not afraid to admit it. Although we didn't have peanut butter cups and similar confections while growing up (they're only now appearing in Croatian stores), I'll always remember when the PB version of Kit Kat was released. My sister and I were just nuts about it. Here, I've switched things up a bit by creating a deliciously soft peanut butter cake and pairing it with light and tangy chocolate cream cheese frosting. *chef's kiss*

Serves 12 to 14

Peanut Butter Cake
Cooking spray or butter, for pans

2 cups (250 g) all-purpose flour

2½ tsp (12 g) baking powder

½ tsp fine sea salt

1 cup (240 ml) buttermilk, at room temperature

3 tbsp (45 ml) sunflower oil

½ tsp vanilla extract

½ cup (1 stick; 115 g) unsalted butter, at room temperature

Rounded ½ cup (150 g) smooth peanut butter

Rounded cup (250 g) soft light brown sugar

3 large eggs, at room temperature

Chocolate Cream Cheese Frosting
5.5 oz (150 g) 55% dark chocolate, finely chopped

7 oz (200 g) cream cheese, cold

Rounded ½ cup (125 g) mascarpone cheese, cold

Scant cup (100 g) powdered sugar, sifted

Rounded ¼ cup (30 g) unsweetened cocoa powder

5 tbsp (75 ml) warm water

1 tsp vanilla extract

1 cup (240 g) heavy cream, cold

Make the cake: Preheat the oven to 350°F (175°C) or 325°F (160°C) if using a fan-assisted oven. Grease three 6-inch (15 cm) round cake pans with cooking spray or butter and line the bottoms with parchment paper.

Sift the flour, baking powder and salt into a medium-sized bowl and whisk to combine. In a measuring jug, lightly whisk together the buttermilk, sunflower oil and vanilla.

Using a stand mixer fitted with the paddle attachment, or a medium-sized bowl if using an electric hand mixer, beat the butter and peanut butter with half of the brown sugar until pale and fluffy, 2 to 3 minutes. Add the rest of the brown sugar and beat to combine. Add the eggs, one at a time, making sure each is fully incorporated before adding the next.

Next, add the flour mixture in three additions, alternating with the buttermilk mixture to avoid splashing and overmixing the batter. After each addition, mix the batter until just combined. Scrape the bowl a couple of times with a silicone spatula to make sure everything is mixed nicely.

Divide the batter equally by weight among the prepared pans and level it with an offset palette knife. Bake for 22 to 25 minutes. It's best to check the cakes after 22 minutes and then adjust the baking time accordingly, because ovens can vary. The cakes are done when they're springy on the top and when a skewer inserted into the middle comes out mostly clean. Remove them from the oven and leave them to cool in their pans on a wire rack for 10 to 15 minutes to firm up a little bit before inverting them onto a wire rack to cool completely.

While the cakes are cooling, prepare the frosting: Melt the chocolate in a heatproof bowl set over a pan of simmering water, then set it aside to slightly cool. In a separate bowl, beat together the cream cheese and mascarpone with the sifted powdered sugar until combined.

In a small bowl, mix the cocoa powder and warm water into a paste, add it to the cream cheese mixture and beat until everything is fully incorporated, then add the melted chocolate along with the vanilla and beat until combined. In a separate bowl, beat the cream to a medium soft peak stage, then gradually fold it into the cheese mixture using a silicone spatula.

(continued)

Peanut Butter **Chocolate Cake** (Continued)

Peanut Brittle

1 cup (200 g) granulated sugar

¼ cup (60 ml) water

1 tbsp (15 g) unsalted butter

1 cup (145 g) roasted and salted peanuts, coarsely chopped

Assemble the cake: Start by leveling the tops of your cakes using a cake leveler or a long, serrated knife for a neater look, if needed. Then, put a little bit of frosting in the middle of a serving plate or your cake board to keep the cake from moving around. Place it on a turntable for easier handling and decorating.

Place one cake layer on the serving plate and, using a small, offset palette knife or a piping bag filled with the frosting, spread the frosting over the top of the cake layer, about ⅜ inch (1 cm) thick. Top it with the next cake layer and repeat the process. Place the final cake layer on top, making sure it's upside down to get a nice, smooth surface on top.

Next, apply a thin layer of frosting around the cake and smooth it using a cake scraper to keep in the crumbs. Chill the cake in the fridge for 30 to 60 minutes before applying the final coat of frosting and decorating.

Once the crumb coat is firm, frost the cake with the remaining frosting in a rustic manner.

Make the peanut brittle: Line a baking sheet with parchment paper or a silicone mat. In a small, heavy-bottomed saucepan, combine the granulated sugar and water. Make sure every sugar granule is covered with water. Bring to a simmer over medium-high heat and continue to cook until it reaches a deep golden amber color. Do not stir the mixture under any circumstance, or else it will crystallize. This can take up to 15 minutes, but I suggest watching over it at all times because caramel burns easily.

When the caramel reaches the desired color, remove the pan from the heat and add the butter, stirring constantly. There will be a lot of bubbles and steam, so be careful not to burn yourself. Once all the bubbles have subsided, add the peanuts and stir quickly until all the peanuts are coated in caramel. Then, pour the mixture onto the prepared baking sheet, spread as evenly as possible into one thin layer and leave it to cool and harden. Once the brittle has hardened, break it into chunks and use it to decorate the cake.

Keep the cake tightly covered in plastic wrap or in an airtight container in the fridge for up to a week, but allow it to come to room temperature before serving.

Banoffe **Chocolate Walnut Cake**

My paternal grandmother used to make this walnut sheet cake that my sister was absolutely obsessed with. Although we haven't eaten it in a very long time, I still remember that it had wonderful walnut frosting, and this cake right here is my homage to that childhood recipe. Here, I've gone the extra mile and made walnut butter instead of just using finely ground walnuts, which lets this frosting keep its silky texture. It also pairs wonderfully with the classic banana and chocolate combination. For the best possible flavor, for the cake layers, use the blackest banana you can find.

. . . .

Serves 12 to 14

Walnut Butter

1½ cups (150 g) walnuts, chopped

1 to 2 tsp (5 to 10 ml) vegetable oil (optional)

Walnut Buttercream

¼ cup + 2 tbsp (45 g) all-purpose flour

1 cup (200 g) granulated sugar

¼ tsp fine sea salt

1½ cups (360 ml) whole milk

1⅓ cups (2⅔ sticks; 300 g) unsalted butter, at room temperature

½ tsp vanilla extract

3 to 4 tbsp (48 to 64 g) walnut butter

Make the walnut butter: In a dry skillet, toast the chopped walnuts over medium-high heat, stirring constantly, until aromatic, about 1 to 2 minutes. Remove them from the heat and let cool for 10 to 15 minutes, then transfer them to a food processor and pulse until the mixture starts to look creamy and smooth, about 2 minutes. If you feel that the processing is taking too long and your food processor might be overheating, add 1 to 2 teaspoons (5 to 10 ml) of vegetable oil to help make the walnut butter smooth and creamy in an instant. Transfer to a clean jar and keep at room temperature until use.

Begin the buttercream: In a small, heavy-bottomed saucepan, whisk together the flour, granulated sugar, salt and milk. Cook over medium to high heat, whisking constantly so the mixture doesn't burn or catch on the bottom of the pan. Once it starts to thicken and you notice bubbling, cook for another 2 minutes, still whisking constantly, until it resembles pastry cream. This whole process could take up to 10 minutes.

When the pudding base is done, strain it through a sieve onto a shallow plate to get rid of any possible lumps. Cover it with plastic wrap touching the surface to prevent a skin from forming and let it cool to room temperature. You can speed up the process by letting it cool in the fridge, but prior to using, it must be room temperature.

(continued)

Chocolate Banana Cake

Cooking spray or butter, for pans

1⅔ cups (200 g) all-purpose flour

Scant ½ cup (50 g) Dutch-processed cocoa powder

2 tsp (10 g) baking powder

¼ tsp ground cinnamon

½ tsp fine sea salt

¼ cup (60 ml) whole milk, at room temperature

Rounded ¾ cup (180 g) sour cream, at room temperature

¼ cup (60 ml) sunflower oil

½ tsp vanilla extract

½ cup (1 stick; 115 g) unsalted butter, at room temperature

¾ cup (150 g) granulated sugar

Scant ½ cup (100 g) soft light brown sugar

2 large eggs, at room temperature

6.5 oz (180 g) mashed overripe banana, at room temperature

Caramelized Bananas

1 large, firm banana, cold

3⅓ tbsp (50 g) light brown sugar

1½ tbsp (23 g) unsalted butter

⅛ tsp cinnamon

Pinch of salt

1 to 2 tbsp (15 to 30 ml) heavy cream or rum (optional)

Make the cake: Preheat the oven to 350°F (175°C) or 325°F (160°C) if using a fan-assisted oven. Grease three 6-inch (15-cm) round cake pans with cooking spray or butter and line the bottoms with parchment paper.

Sift the flour, cocoa powder, baking powder, cinnamon and salt into a medium-sized bowl and whisk to combine. In a measuring jug, lightly whisk together the milk, sour cream, sunflower oil and vanilla.

Using a stand mixer fitted with the paddle attachment, or a medium-sized bowl if using an electric hand mixer, beat the butter with half of both sugars until pale and fluffy, about 2 to 3 minutes. Add the rest of both sugars and beat to combine. Add the eggs, one at a time, making sure making sure the first egg is fully incorporated before adding the second. Add the mashed banana and mix until combined.

Next, add the flour mixture in three additions, alternating with the sour cream mixture to avoid splashing and overmixing the batter. After each addition, mix the batter until just combined. Scrape the bowl a couple of times with a silicone spatula to make sure everything is mixed nicely.

Divide the batter equally by weight among the prepared pans and level with an offset palette knife, then bake for 22 to 25 minutes. It's best to check the cakes after 22 minutes and then adjust the baking time accordingly, because ovens can vary. The cakes are done if they spring back when lightly touched and when a skewer inserted into the middle comes out mostly clean. Remove the cakes from the oven and leave them to cool in their pans on a wire rack for 10 to 15 minutes to firm up a little bit, then remove them from the pans to cool completely.

While the cakes are cooling, finish the buttercream: Using the stand mixer fitted with the paddle attachment, beat the butter for 5 minutes, or until it's pale and fluffy. Then, add the previously made pudding base, one spoonful at a time. Beat everything until nicely incorporated with no lumps. Lastly, add the vanilla and walnut butter and beat for a couple of seconds, until smooth and combined. If the frosting seems a little soft, put it in the fridge to firm up a little bit.

Cut the cold, firm banana into ½-inch (6-mm) round slices and set aside. In a medium-sized skillet, stirring occasionally, heat the light brown sugar with the butter, cinnamon and salt, until the mixture is melted, homogenous and starts bubbling. Carefully add the bananas, spaced evenly, and cook over medium heat, without stirring, for about 2 to 3 minutes on each side. They're done when the bananas are browned and caramelized, but not mushy. If the sauce becomes too sticky or too dark, add a couple of tablespoons (30 ml) of heavy cream or rum and carefully stir to combine. Remove from the heat and set aside until needed.

(continued)

Chocolate Ganache

2 oz (60 g) 55% dark chocolate, finely chopped

⅓ cup (70 g) heavy cream

Banana chips, for decorating (optional)

Assemble the cake: Start by leveling the tops of your cakes using a cake leveler or a long, serrated knife for a neater look, if needed. Then, put a little bit of buttercream in the middle of a serving plate or your cake board to keep the cake from moving around. Place it on a turntable for easier handling and decorating.

Place one cake layer on the serving plate and, using a small, offset palette knife or a piping bag filled with buttercream, spread the frosting over the top of the cake layer, about ¼ inch (6 mm) thick. Make a dam of frosting around the outer edge of the top of the cake and fill with caramelized bananas. Top it with the next cake layer and repeat the process. Place the final cake layer on top, making sure it's upside down to get a nice, smooth surface on top.

Next, apply a thin layer of frosting around the sides of the cake and smooth it using a cake scraper to keep in the crumbs. Chill the cake in the fridge for 30 to 60 minutes before applying the final coat of frosting and decorating.

Once the crumb coat is firm, frost the cake with the remaining buttercream and smooth the sides using a decorative cake scraper (cake comb). Chill the cake for 30 to 60 minutes.

Make the chocolate ganache: Place the chocolate in a small, heatproof bowl. In a small saucepan, bring the cream to a simmer, then pour it over the chocolate. Cover with a plate and let it sit for 1 to 2 minutes, or until the chocolate softens and begins to melt. Stir with a spatula until combined and smooth. Alternatively, you can do this (using a microwave-safe bowl) in a microwave in 30-second intervals. If it seems too loose, leave it to cool and thicken for 10 to 15 minutes before pouring over the chilled cake.

When your cake is chilled and you're ready to decorate, pour two-thirds of the chocolate ganache onto the middle of your cake and slowly spread it around with a small, offset palette knife for a natural-looking drip. If you need more, add the remaining third of the ganache on top and spread it in the same manner. The final quantity needed depends on how thick the ganache is and how chilled the cake is. You might end up with a little leftover ganache.

Put the cake in the fridge so the chocolate drip has time to set. After that, place the buttercream in a piping bag fitted with a round nozzle and pipe some buttercream across the center of the top of the cake. Decorate with banana chips, if desired.

The cake is best when served and eaten at room temperature. You can keep the cake in the fridge, covered in plastic wrap or in an airtight container, but take it out of the fridge at least an hour before serving.

Cookie Dough **Brownie Cake**

Talk about an indulgent dessert, am I right? Merging my two great loves resulted in this exceptionally rich cake. You might be thinking it's just like a brookie, but the edible cookie dough stays just a little bit soft, thanks to the sticky condensed milk. The brownie cake is very chocolaty and dense from using both chocolate and cocoa powder, and to provide a bit of lightness to an otherwise chocolate bomb, the cake is topped with barely sweetened Chantilly cream.

. . . .

Serves 10 to 12

Edible Cookie Dough
Scant 1⅓ cups (160 g) all-purpose flour

⅔ cup (150 g) soft light brown sugar

½ cup (1 stick; 115 g) unsalted butter, at room temperature

3.5 oz (100 g) condensed milk

1 tsp vanilla extract

½ tsp fine sea salt

5.5 oz (150 g) 55% dark chocolate, finely chopped

Brownie Cake
Cooking spray or butter, for pan

3.5 oz (100 g) 60% dark chocolate, finely chopped

Rounded ¼ cup (35 g) Dutch-processed cocoa powder, sifted

¼ cup + 1 tsp (75 g) hot water

Rounded ¾ cup (100 g) all-purpose flour

1 tsp baking powder

Scant ⅔ cup (120 g) granulated sugar

¼ cup (60 g) soft light brown sugar

½ tsp fine sea salt

⅔ cup (1⅓ sticks; 150 g) unsalted butter, at room temperature

⅓ cup + 1½ tbsp (100 g) sour cream, at room temperature

2 large eggs, at room temperature

½ tsp vanilla extract

Make the edible cookie dough: In a dry skillet, toast the flour over medium-high heat for 5 to 6 minutes, or until slightly golden. Remove from the heat and let cool.

In a medium-sized bowl, beat together the sugar and butter, using an electric hand mixer, until pale, fluffy and combined, about 3 minutes. Add the condensed milk, vanilla and salt, and beat until fully incorporated. Sift the toasted flour into the bowl and beat on low speed until just combined. Lastly, fold in the chocolate. The dough will be a little sticky to work with, so cover the bowl with plastic wrap and place in the fridge until needed.

Make the cake: Preheat the oven to 350°F (175°C) or 325°F (160°C) if using a fan-assisted oven. Lightly grease a 9-inch (23-cm) round springform pan with cooking spray or butter and line the base with parchment paper.

Place the chocolate in a small, heatproof bowl. Melt over a pan of simmering water, making sure the bowl doesn't touch the water. Set aside to cool slightly.

In a small bowl, combine the sifted cocoa powder with hot water using a whisk, until smooth and creamy. Allow it to cool a little bit before using. Sift the flour, baking powder, granulated and brown sugars and salt into the bowl of a stand mixer fitted with the paddle attachment and whisk to combine. Add the butter and mix on low speed until you get a sandlike texture and there are no traces of flour. Next, add the sour cream, bloomed cocoa powder, eggs, vanilla and melted chocolate and beat on low speed until fully incorporated.

(continued)

Cookie Dough **Brownie Cake** (Continued)

Chantilly Cream

Scant 1½ cups (360 g) heavy cream, cold

¼ cup (30 g) powdered sugar, sifted

1 tsp vanilla extract

Scrape the batter into the prepared pan and spread evenly. Take the edible cookie dough out of the fridge, form eight 2-tablespoon (30-g) balls and push them halfway down into the batter all along the inside edge of the springform pan, with one cookie dough ball being in the middle. Save any leftover cookie dough for decoration later.

Bake the cake for 30 to 35 minutes, or until a skewer inserted into the middle (make sure to hit the cake and not the cookie dough) comes out with a few moist crumbs. Remove from the oven and leave to cool in the pan for 10 minutes before removing from the pan to cool completely.

Make the Chantilly cream: In a large bowl, using an electric mixer, beat together the cold cream, powdered sugar and vanilla until the mixture reaches soft peaks. Spread the cream over the cake in a rustic manner using a spoon, and top with little nuggets of leftover cookie dough.

This cake is best when served the same day, but you can keep it in the fridge in an airtight container for up to a week, just let it come to room temperature at least half an hour before serving.

Chocolate *Orange* Bundt Cake

Are you familiar with Jaffa cakes? Well, this cake resembles that little biscuit quite a lot. If there's anything you should know about my family's taste preferences, it's that we love the addition of orange zest in almost anything. Ganache? Do it. Pancakes? Do it. Chocolate chip cookies? Do it. In this rich and moist chocolate cake, I used both freshly squeezed orange juice and zest for maximum orange flavor, and it came out beautifully sweet and refreshing at the same time. The chocolate glaze makes it that much more luxurious, but feel free to make a simple orange icing instead if that's your preference.

. . . .

Serves 12 to 14

Cake
Cooking spray or butter, for pans

Rounded 1¾ cups (225 g) all-purpose flour

⅔ cup (75 g) Dutch-processed cocoa powder

2½ tsp (12 g) baking powder

1 cup (200 g) granulated sugar

⅔ cup (150 g) light brown sugar

½ tsp fine sea salt

1¼ cups (300 g) sour cream, at room temperature

Zest of 2 oranges

½ cup (120 ml) fresh orange juice

⅔ cup (160 ml) sunflower oil

2 large eggs, at room temperature

1 tsp vanilla extract

Chocolate Glaze
3.5 oz (100 g) 55% dark chocolate, finely chopped

Zest of 1 orange

½ cup (120 ml) heavy cream

Candied orange peel, for decorating

Make the cake: Preheat the oven to 350°F (175°C) or 325°F (160°C) if using a fan-assisted oven. Grease a 10-cup (2.4-L) Bundt pan with cooking spray or butter.

Sift the flour, cocoa powder, baking powder, granulated and brown sugars and salt into the bowl of a stand mixer fitted with the paddle attachment, or a medium-sized bowl if you're using an electric hand mixer, and whisk to combine. In a measuring jug, lightly whisk together the sour cream, orange zest and juice, sunflower oil, eggs and vanilla.

Add the sour cream mixture to the flour mixture in three equal batches to avoid splashing and overmixing the batter. After each addition, mix the batter for about 15 seconds, or until everything is fully incorporated. Scrape the bowl a couple of times with a silicone spatula to make sure everything is mixed nicely. Don't overmix the batter.

Scrape the batter into the prepared pan and bake for 45 to 50 minutes, or until a skewer inserted into the middle comes out mostly clean. It's best to check the cake after 40 minutes and then adjust the baking time accordingly, because ovens can vary. When the cake is done, remove it from the oven and allow it to cool in the pan for 15 minutes before carefully inverting it onto a wire rack to cool completely.

Make the chocolate glaze: Place the chocolate and orange zest in a heatproof bowl. In a small saucepan, bring the cream to a simmer, then pour it over the chocolate mixture. Cover it with a plate and let sit for 1 to 2 minutes, then stir the mixture with a spatula until combined and smooth.

Once the cake is cooled, transfer it to a serving plate and pour the chocolate glaze over it. If desired, top the cake with some candied orange peel.

Store the cake in an airtight container at room temperature for up to 2 days, or for up to 5 days in the fridge. Allow it to come to room temperature before serving.

Note: For an all-chocolate Bundt cake, replace the orange juice with whole milk and omit the orange zest.

Strawberry Chocolate Sheet Cake

They say chocolate and strawberries are a match made in heaven, and I can't disagree. In this recipe, the sweet, fresh flavor of the homemade strawberry jam mixed with my favorite ermine buttercream gives you a delicious flavor that tastes almost like strawberry ice cream. It's the perfect topping for the incredibly chocolaty and moist sheet cake, and is sure to satisfy any crowd.

. . . .

Serves 16 to 18

Strawberry Jam
17.5 oz (500 g) fresh or frozen strawberries

¾ cup (150 g) granulated sugar

1 tbsp (15 g) fresh lemon juice

Strawberry Buttercream
Rounded ¼ cup (35 g) all-purpose flour

¾ cup (150 g) granulated sugar

¼ tsp fine sea salt

1⅛ cups (280 g) whole milk

1⅛ cups (2¼ sticks; 250 g) unsalted butter, at room temperature

4 to 5 tbsp (60 to 75 ml) strawberry jam

Chocolate Cake
Cooking spray or butter, for pans

Rounded 1¾ cups (230 g) all-purpose flour

Scant cup (100 g) unsweetened cocoa powder

2¾ tsp (14 g) baking powder

1½ cups (350 g) soft light brown sugar

½ tsp fine sea salt

Rounded cup (240 g) sour cream, at room temperature

¾ cup (180 ml) sunflower oil

3 medium-sized eggs, at room temperature

1 tsp vanilla extract

⅔ cup (160 ml) hot water

Make the strawberry jam: In a medium-sized saucepan, combine the strawberries and granulated sugar. Bring to a simmer over medium-high heat, stirring occasionally so the jam doesn't catch on the bottom of the pan. Press the strawberries with the back of the silicone spatula or a wooden spoon to speed up the process. Simmer until the mixture is thick, 15 to 20 minutes, then remove from the heat, add the lemon juice and puree with an immersion blender until smooth. Transfer the jam to a jar and place it in the fridge to cool completely.

Begin the buttercream: In a small, heavy-bottomed saucepan, whisk together the flour, sugar, salt and milk. Cook over medium to high heat, whisking constantly so the mixture doesn't burn or catch on the bottom of the pan. Once it starts to thicken and you notice bubbling, cook for another 2 minutes, still whisking constantly, until it resembles pastry cream. This could take about 10 minutes.

When the pudding base is done, strain it through a sieve onto a shallow plate to get rid of any possible lumps. Cover it with plastic wrap touching the surface to prevent a skin from forming and let cool to room temperature. You can speed up the process by letting it cool in the fridge, but prior to mixing it with the butter, it must be at room temperature.

Make the cake: Preheat the oven to 350°F (175°C) or 325°F (160°C) if using a fan-assisted oven. Lightly grease a 9 x 13–inch (23 x 33–cm) baking pan with cooking spray or butter and line it with parchment paper that hangs over the 2 long sides for easier handling later.

Sift the flour, cocoa powder, baking powder, brown sugar and salt into a large bowl and whisk to combine. In a measuring jug, lightly whisk together the sour cream, sunflower oil, eggs and vanilla. Add the sour cream mixture to the flour mixture and whisk to combine into a thick batter. Add the hot water in two or three additions and whisk until smooth.

Pour the batter into the prepared pan and spread evenly. Bake for 35 to 40 minutes. The cake is done if it springs back when lightly touched and when a skewer inserted into the middle comes out mostly clean. Remove the cake from the oven and leave to cool in the pan for 15 to 20 minutes to firm up before transferring to a wire rack to cool completely.

(continued)

11 oz (300 g) fresh strawberries, for decorating

While the cake is cooling, finish the buttercream: Using the stand mixer fitted with the paddle attachment, beat the butter for 5 to 6 minutes, or until it's pale and fluffy. Then, add the previously made pudding base, one spoonful at a time. Beat everything until nicely incorporated with no lumps. Lastly, add the strawberry jam and beat until smooth and combined.

Spread the frosting over the cooled cake and top with the fresh strawberries.

Keep the cake covered in the fridge for up to 1 week. Before serving, allow it to come to room temperature.

Note: Leftover jam will last for 2 to 3 weeks in the fridge. You can use it in a smoothie bowl or as a crepe filling (see page 93).

Chocolate Pretzel *Caramel* Cake

Salty and sweet combinations are my weakness. Adding a buttery pretzel crust to the cake layers in this recipe provides not only a delicious crunchy element, but a wonderful salty contrast to the sweet, fluffy and moist chocolate cake. The salted caramel filling and frosting bind it all together into a rich, decadent chocolate dessert worthy of every chocoholic.

. . . .

Serves 12 to 14

Salted Caramel Sauce
1 cup (200 g) granulated sugar

¼ cup (60 g) water

¾ cup (180 ml) heavy cream

½ tsp vanilla extract

¾ tsp fine sea salt

Salted Caramel Buttercream
⅓ cup (40 g) all-purpose flour

¾ cup (150 g) granulated sugar

¼ tsp fine sea salt

1½ cups (360 ml) whole milk

1⅓ cups (2⅔ sticks; 300 g) unsalted butter, at room temperature

½ tsp vanilla extract

4 to 5 tbsp (60 to 75 ml) salted caramel sauce

Salted Pretzel Base
Cooking spray or butter, for pans

3 cups (195 g) salted pretzels

6 tbsp (105 g) unsalted butter, melted

3 tbsp (45 g) soft light brown sugar

Make the salted caramel sauce: In a small, heavy-bottomed saucepan, combine the granulated sugar and water. Make sure every sugar granule is covered with water. Bring to a simmer over medium-high heat and continue to cook until it reaches a golden amber color. Do not stir the mixture under any circumstance, because it will crystallize. This can take about 15 minutes, but I suggest watching it the entire time because caramel burns easily.

While the sugar is dissolving, in a separate small saucepan, bring the cream and vanilla to a simmer. Once the sugar syrup reaches the desired color, remove it from the heat and pour the cream mixture over it in a slow and steady stream, stirring constantly with a silicone spatula. There will be a lot of bubbles and steam, so be careful not to burn yourself.

Once all the bubbles have subsided, put the sauce back on the stove, over medium heat, and cook it for a minute, stirring constantly. When it's done, stir in the salt and transfer to a clean jar to cool to room temperature.

Begin the buttercream: In a small, heavy-bottomed saucepan, whisk together the flour, granulated sugar, salt and milk. Cook over medium to high heat, whisking constantly so it doesn't burn or catch on the bottom of the pan. Once it starts to thicken and you notice bubbling, cook for another 1 to 2 minutes, still whisking constantly, until it resembles pastry cream. This could take about 10 minutes.

When the pudding base is done, strain it through a sieve onto a shallow plate to get rid of any possible lumps. Cover it with plastic wrap touching the surface to prevent a skin from forming and let it cool to room temperature. You can speed up the process by letting it cool in the fridge, but prior to using, it must be room temperature.

Make the pretzel base: Preheat the oven to 350°F (175°C) or 325°F (160°C) if using a fan-assisted oven. Grease three 6-inch (15-cm) round cake pans with cooking spray or butter and line the bottoms with parchment paper.

In a food processor, pulse the pretzels until finely ground. Add the melted butter and brown sugar and pulse until evenly combined. Divide the mixture equally into the prepared pans and press firmly to create an even layer. Bake for 6 to 7 minutes, then remove from the oven and set aside. Leave the oven on at the temperature it has been set to.

(continued)

Chocolate Pretzel *Caramel* Cake (Continued)

Chocolate Cake

Scant 1½ cups (180 g) all-purpose flour

⅔ cup (75 g) Dutch-processed cocoa powder

2¼ tsp (11.5 g) baking powder

¾ cup (150 g) granulated sugar

⅔ cup (150 g) soft light brown sugar

½ tsp fine sea salt

Rounded ¾ cup (180 g) sour cream, at room temperature

½ cup (120 ml) sunflower oil

2 large eggs, at room temperature

1 tsp vanilla extract

½ cup + 1 tbsp (135 ml) hot water

About ½ cup (about 50 g) crushed pretzels (optional), plus some whole pretzels

Make the cake: Sift the flour, cocoa powder, baking powder, granulated and brown sugars and salt into a large bowl and whisk to combine. In a measuring jug, lightly whisk together the sour cream, sunflower oil, eggs and vanilla and lightly mix them together using a whisk. Add the sour cream mixture to the flour mixture and whisk to combine into a thick batter. Lastly, add the hot water in two to three additions and whisk until smooth.

Divide the batter equally by weight among the prepared pans and level it with an offset palette knife. Bake for 23 to 28 minutes. It's best to check the cakes after 23 minutes and then adjust the baking time accordingly, because ovens can vary. The cakes are done if they spring back when lightly touched and when a skewer inserted into the middle comes out mostly clean. Remove from the oven and leave to cool in the pan for 10 minutes to firm up before transferring onto a wire rack to cool completely.

While the cakes are cooling, finish the buttercream: Use a stand mixer fitted with the paddle attachment to beat the butter for 5 minutes, or until it's pale and fluffy. Then, add the previously made pudding spoonful by spoonful. Beat everything until nicely incorporated with no lumps. Lastly, add the vanilla and salted caramel sauce and beat until smooth and fully combined.

Assemble the cake: Start by leveling the tops of your cakes using a cake leveler or a long, serrated knife for a neater look, if needed. Then, put a little bit of buttercream in the middle of a serving plate or your cake board to keep the cake from moving around. Place it on a turntable for easier handling and decorating.

Place one cake layer on the serving plate and, using a small, offset palette knife or a piping bag filled with buttercream, spread the frosting over the top of the cake layer, ⅜ inch (1 cm) thick. Make a dam or border around the edges and fill with some salted caramel sauce. Top it with the next cake layer and repeat the process.

Place the final cake layer on top and then apply a thin layer of frosting around the sides and the top of the cake. Smooth it using a cake scraper to keep in the crumbs. Chill the cake in the fridge for 30 to 60 minutes before applying the final coat of frosting and decorating.

Once the crumb coat is firm, frost the cake with the remaining buttercream, smooth the sides, then make a swirl effect using a small offset palette knife, while leaving the top completely smooth. Gently apply crushed pretzels (if using) at the bottom of the cake and put in the fridge for 20 to 30 minutes before adding the final touches.

(continued)

Chocolate Pretzel *Caramel* Cake (Continued)

Chocolate Ganache

2 oz (60 g) 55% dark chocolate, finely chopped

⅓ cup (70 g) heavy cream

Make the chocolate ganache: Place the chocolate in a small, heatproof bowl. In a small saucepan, bring the cream to a simmer, then pour it over the chocolate. Cover with a plate and let sit for 1 to 2 minutes, or until the chocolate softens and begins to melt. Stir with a spatula until combined and smooth. Alternatively, you can do this (using a microwave-safe bowl) in a microwave in 30-second intervals. If the ganache seems too loose, leave it to cool and thicken for about 10 to 15 minutes before pouring over the chilled cake.

When your cake is chilled and you're ready to decorate, pour two-thirds of the chocolate ganache onto the middle of your cake and slowly spread it around with a small offset palette knife for a natural-looking drip. If you need more, add the remaining third of the ganache on top and spread it in the same manner. The final quantity needed depends on how thick the ganache is and how chilled the cake is. You might end up with a little leftover ganache.

Put the cake in the fridge so the chocolate drip has time to set. Then, decorate the cake with any leftover buttercream placed in a piping bag fitted with a big star nozzle and extra pretzels.

Keep the cake tightly covered in plastic wrap or in an airtight container at room temperature for 2 days or in the fridge for up to a week. Allow it to come to room temperature before serving.

Passion Fruit Milk Chocolate Cupcakes

Inspired by Pierre Hermé's famous macaron flavor, I decided to pair a refreshing, tropical passion fruit buttercream with sweet chocolate cupcakes—and wow, what a delicious, unique combination this turned out to be! I call them milk chocolate cupcakes, because I use a milder version of chocolate batter, enhancing the milky flavor with evaporated milk.

. . . .

Serves 12 to 14

Passion Fruit Curd
7 oz (200 g) passion fruit puree

2 tbsp (30 ml) fresh lemon juice

Scant ⅔ cup (125 g) sugar

Pinch of salt

5 large egg yolks

⅓ cup (⅔ stick; 75 g) unsalted butter, cubed, cold

Passion Fruit Buttercream
3 tbsp (25 g) all-purpose flour

½ cup + 1½ tbsp (120 g) granulated sugar

Pinch of salt

¾ cup + 1 tbsp (195 ml) whole milk

13 tbsp (185 g) unsalted butter, at room temperature

4 to 5 tbsp (56 to 70 g) passion fruit curd

Milk Chocolate Cupcakes
Scant 1½ cups (180 g) all-purpose flour

Rounded ¼ cup (30 g) Dutch-processed cocoa powder

2 tsp (10 g) baking powder

½ tsp fine sea salt

1 cup + 2 lbsp (225 g) granulated sugar

½ cup (120 g) evaporated milk

½ cup (120 g) sour cream, at room temperature

3 tbsp (45 ml) sunflower oil

2 large eggs, at room temperature

½ tsp vanilla extract

⅓ cup (⅔ stick; 75 g) unsalted butter, at room temperature

Make the passion fruit curd: In a small heavy-bottomed saucepan, whisk together the passion fruit puree, lemon juice, sugar, salt and egg yolks. Cook over medium-low heat, whisking constantly, until it thickens, 10 to 15 minutes. The curd is ready when it can coat the back of a wooden spoon. Once it's done, add the butter and whisk until everything is incorporated and smooth. Strain the curd through a sieve to get rid of any possible lumps and transfer to a glass jar. Refrigerate for a couple of hours, or until it comes to a spreadable consistency.

Begin the buttercream: In a small, heavy-bottomed saucepan, whisk together the flour, sugar, salt and milk. Cook over medium to high heat, whisking constantly so the mixture doesn't burn or catch on the bottom of the pan. Once it starts to thicken and you notice bubbling, cook for another 2 minutes, still whisking constantly, until it resembles pastry cream. This whole process could take up to 10 minutes.

When the pudding base is done, strain it through a sieve onto a shallow plate to get rid of any possible lumps. Cover it with plastic wrap touching the surface to prevent a skin from forming and let it cool to room temperature. You can speed up the process by letting it cool in the fridge, but prior to using, it must be room temperature.

Make the cupcakes: Preheat the oven to 350°F (175°C) or 325°F (160°C) if using a fan-assisted oven. Line a cupcake pan with 12 paper liners.

Sift the flour, cocoa powder, baking powder and salt into a medium-sized bowl. Add the sugar and whisk to combine. In a measuring jug, lightly whisk together the evaporated milk, sour cream, sunflower oil, eggs and vanilla. Add the butter to the flour mixture, fit the stand mixer with the paddle attachment and mix on low speed until you get a sandlike texture and there are no traces of flour.

Next, add the evaporated milk mixture in two equal batches to avoid splashing and overmixing the batter. After each addition, mix the batter on low speed for about 15 seconds, or until everything is fully incorporated. Scrape the bowl a couple of times with a silicone spatula to make sure everything is mixed nicely.

(continued)

Passion Fruit Milk Chocolate Cupcakes
(Continued)

Fill the prepared paper liners three-quarters of the way full and bake for 18 to 20 minutes. The cupcakes are done if they spring back when lightly touched or when a toothpick inserted into the middle of a cupcake comes out mostly clean.

Remove the cupcakes from the oven and let them firm up in the pan for 2 to 3 minutes before transferring them to a wire rack to cool completely.

While the cupcakes are cooling, finish the buttercream: Using the stand mixer fitted with the paddle attachment, beat the butter for 5 minutes, or until it's pale and fluffy, then add the previously made pudding base, one spoonful at a time. Beat everything until nicely incorporated with no lumps. Lastly, add the passion fruit curd and beat for a couple of seconds, until smooth and combined.

Assemble the cupcakes: Make a hole in the center of each cupcake using an apple corer or small spoon, and fill with the remaining passion fruit curd. Transfer the buttercream to a piping bag fitted with a big open star nozzle and make swirls on top of the cupcakes.

The cupcakes are best when served the same day at room temperature, but you can keep them in the fridge in an airtight container for 2 to 3 days.

> **Note:** To make the passion fruit curd I use good-quality store-bought passion fruit puree, because it's difficult for me to find fresh passion fruit. If the curd doesn't start thickening, you can always add 1 to 2 teaspoons (2 to 4 g) of cornstarch diluted with a little water to salvage it.

Caramelized White Chocolate Hazelnut Cake

If you still haven't had the chance to try caramelized white chocolate, then prepare yourself to be amazed. Even though it requires a little bit of prep time, I promise it's very easy to make, and most of all, so worth it. With its toasty, caramel notes, it makes the most wonderful sweet, almost nutty frosting that elevates pretty much any dessert and leaves people wondering what that incredible flavor is. Here I chose to pair it with one of my favorites—hazelnut cake—but it would go brilliantly with a simple vanilla or chocolate cake, too.

· ·

Serves 12 to 14

Caramelized White Chocolate
14 oz (400 g) white chocolate, at least 28%, chopped

Caramelized White Chocolate Buttercream
⅓ cup (40 g) all-purpose flour

½ cup + 2 tbsp (130 g) granulated sugar

¼ tsp fine sea salt

1½ cups (360 ml) whole milk

5.5 oz (150 g) caramelized white chocolate

⅓ cup (2⅔ sticks; 300 g) unsalted butter, at room temperature

½ tsp vanilla extract

Hazelnut Vanilla Cake
Cooking spray or butter, for pans

2 cups (250 g) all-purpose flour

2 tsp (10 g) baking powder

½ tsp fine sea salt

Rounded ¾ cup (180 g) sour cream, at room temperature

½ tsp vanilla extract

½ cup (1 stick; 115 g) unsalted butter, at room temperature

½ cup (100 g) granulated sugar

⅔ cup (150 g) soft light brown sugar

3.5 oz (100 g) Hazelnut Butter (page 19)

3 large eggs, at room temperature

Caramelize the white chocolate: Preheat the oven to 275°F (140°C) or 250°F (120°C) if using a fan-assisted oven. On a rimmed baking sheet, arrange the white chocolate evenly in a single layer and bake for 60 to 90 minutes, scraping every 10 minutes with a silicone spatula so it caramelizes evenly and doesn't burn. Be careful not to burn it, and don't skip this step. It will go through various grainy stages, but just keep going until it's smooth, creamy and the color of peanut butter.

Once it's done, pour it into a container lined with parchment paper and place in the fridge. Since the chocolate isn't tempered, this is the only way to quickly harden it to be able to break into chunks to melt later.

Begin the buttercream: In a small, heavy-bottomed saucepan, whisk together the flour, granulated sugar, salt and milk. Cook over medium to high heat, whisking constantly so the mixture doesn't burn or catch on the bottom of the pan. Once it starts to thicken and you notice bubbling, cook for another 1 to 2 minutes, still whisking constantly, until it resembles pastry cream. This whole process could take up to 10 minutes.

When the pudding base is done, strain it through a sieve onto a shallow plate to get rid of any possible lumps. Cover it with plastic wrap touching the surface to prevent a skin from forming and let it cool to room temperature. You can speed up the process by letting it cool in the fridge, but prior to using, it must be room temperature.

Make the cake: Preheat the oven to 350°F (175°C) or 325°F (160°C) if using a fan-assisted oven. Grease three 6-inch (15-cm) round cake pans with cooking spray or butter and line the bottoms with parchment paper.

Sift the flour, baking powder and salt into a medium-sized bowl and whisk to combine. In a measuring jug, lightly whisk together the sour cream and vanilla.

Using a stand mixer fitted with the paddle attachment, beat the butter with the granulated sugar until pale and fluffy, 2 to 3 minutes. Add the brown sugar and hazelnut butter and beat to combine. Add the eggs, one at a time, making sure each is fully incorporated before adding the next.

(continued)

Next, add the flour mixture in three additions, alternating with the sour cream mixture to avoid splashing and overmixing the batter. After each addition, mix the batter just until combined. Scrape the bowl a couple of times with a silicone spatula to make sure everything is mixed nicely.

Divide the batter equally by weight among the prepared pans and level with an offset palette knife, then bake for 22 to 25 minutes. It's best to check the cakes after 22 minutes and then adjust the baking time accordingly, because ovens can vary. The cakes are done if they spring back when lightly touched and when a skewer inserted into the middle comes out mostly clean. Remove from the oven and leave them to cool in their pans on a wire rack for 10 to 15 minutes to firm up a little bit before removing them from the pans to cool completely.

While the cakes are cooling, finish the buttercream: Melt 5.5 ounces (150 g) of the caramelized white chocolate in a small, heatproof bowl set over a pan of simmering water. Set aside to slightly cool.

Using the stand mixer fitted with the paddle attachment, beat the butter for 5 minutes, or until it's pale and fluffy, then add the previously made pudding base, one spoonful at a time. Beat everything until nicely incorporated with no lumps. Lastly, add the vanilla and the melted chocolate and beat until smooth and combined.

Assemble the cake: Start by leveling the tops of your cakes using a cake leveler or a long, serrated knife for a neater look, if needed. Then, put a little bit of buttercream in the middle of a serving plate or cake board to keep the cake from moving around. Place it on a turntable for easier handling and decorating.

Place one cake layer on the serving plate and, using a small, offset palette knife or a piping bag filled with buttercream, spread the frosting over the top of the cake layer, about ⅜ inch (1 cm) thick. Top it with the next cake layer and repeat the process. Place the final cake layer on top, making sure it's upside down to get a nice, smooth surface on top.

Next, apply a thin layer of frosting around the cake and smooth it using a cake scraper to keep in the crumbs. Chill the cake in the fridge for 30 to 60 minutes before applying the final coat of frosting and decorating.

Once the crumb coat is firm, frost the cake with the remaining buttercream and smooth it using a cake scraper. Chill the cake for 30 to 60 minutes before putting the chocolate drip on top.

Caramelized White Chocolate Ganache

2.5 oz (75 g) caramelized white chocolate, finely chopped

¼ cup (60 g) heavy cream

Roasted hazelnuts, for decorating (optional)

Make the caramelized white chocolate ganache: Finely chop the caramelized white chocolate in a small, heatproof bowl. In a small saucepan, bring the cream to a simmer, then pour it over the chocolate. Cover with a plate and let sit for 1 to 2 minutes, or until the chocolate softens and begins to melt. Stir with a spatula until combined and smooth. Alternatively, you can do this (using a microwave-safe bowl) in a microwave in 30-second intervals. If it seems too loose, leave it to cool and thicken for 10 to 15 minutes before pouring over the chilled cake.

When your cake is chilled and you're ready to decorate, pour two-thirds of the ganache onto the middle of your cake and slowly spread it around with a small offset palette knife for a natural-looking drip. If you need more, add the remaining third of the ganache on top and spread it in the same manner. The final quantity needed depends on how thick the ganache is and how chilled the cake is. You might end up with a little leftover ganache.

Put the cake in the fridge so the chocolate drip has time to set. Then, decorate the top of the cake by making a buttercream rope border on top and, if desired, sprinkle some chopped, roasted hazelnuts on top or the sides of the cake.

Keep the cake tightly covered in plastic wrap or in an airtight container at room temperature for 2 days or in the fridge for up to a week. Allow it to come to room temperature before serving.

Chocolate *Cookie Butter* Cheesecake

Cookie butter is a sweet spread, made from speculoos cookies, which has become extremely popular in the last couple of years, and it's not difficult to understand why. Its spicy, caramel-like aroma pairs wonderfully with a lot of classic flavors, including this delicious and creamy baked chocolate cheesecake. The most famous cookie butter is the one made from Belgian Biscoff cookies, but you can use any kind of speculoos cookie butter you like.

Serves 10 to 12

Crust
Cooking spray or butter, for pan

9 oz (250 g) speculoos cookies

½ cup + 2 tsp (1 stick + 2 tsp; 125 g) unsalted butter, melted

Cheesecake Filling
9 oz (250 g) 60% dark chocolate, finely chopped

1½ lb (680 g) full-fat cream cheese, at room temperature

Rounded ¾ cup (180 g) sour cream, at room temperature

⅔ cup (150 g) soft light brown sugar

1 tsp vanilla extract

4 large eggs, at room temperature

6.6 oz (200 g) cookie butter, warmed, to top

Make the crust: Preheat the oven to 350°F (175°C) or 325°F (160°C) if using a fan-assisted oven. Lightly grease a 9-inch (23-cm) round springform pan with cooking spray or butter and line the base with parchment paper.

In a food processor, pulse the speculoos cookies until finely ground. Add the melted butter and pulse until evenly combined. Transfer the mixture to the prepared pan and press firmly to create an even layer, pressing a little up the sides as well. Bake the crust for 10 minutes, then remove from the oven and set aside.

Make the filling: Place the chocolate in a small, heatproof bowl set over a pan of simmering water, stirring with a spatula to melt. Set aside to cool slightly.

In a large bowl, combine the cream cheese, sour cream, brown sugar and vanilla and beat using an electric hand mixer until smooth. Add the melted chocolate and beat until there are no white streaks. Add the eggs, one at a time, making sure each is fully incorporated before adding the next. Scrape the bowl a couple of times with a silicone spatula to make sure everything is mixed nicely.

Pour the filling over the crust and spread into an even layer. Bake for 35 to 40 minutes, or until set around the edges, with a slight wobble in the middle. Remove the cheesecake from the oven and leave in the pan on a wire rack to cool to room temperature before putting it in the fridge to cool completely, at least 4 hours. Before serving, top the cheesecake with warmed cookie butter.

Keep your cheesecake, covered, in the fridge for 3 to 4 days.

Note: To reduce the chance of your cheesecake cracking, place a pan filled with hot water on the lowest oven rack to create steamy atmosphere, and make sure not to overbake the cheesecake.

Spring Blossoms

All the zingy fruit and floral combinations in this chapter speak springtime to me, despite some of them not actually blooming during spring. But that's okay—after all, baking is all about the feeling, right?

I fell in love with rosewater as a kid through the flavor of traditional Croatian Easter bread called *pinca*. That's why it's no wonder that rose has sneaked its way into two recipes in this chapter. One of them is a traditional Middle Eastern flavor combination in the Rose Pistachio Cake (page 52) that is now a family favorite, and the second is the Raspberry Rose Loaf Cake (page 66)—an easy dessert recipe that is still a total showstopper.

Aside from using extracts where necessary, we'll bring flavors to life by making quick fruit jams or infusing milk with tea, which is my favorite way to add a delicious boost of flavor to any recipe.

Don't skip the lovely Earl Grey flavor in the Earl Grey Blackberry White Chocolate Cake (page 63), which would make a wonderful addition to any party. And for all my cheesecake lovers out there, I've included my signature lemon cheesecake, but this time I made it even better with the addition of homemade blueberry pie filling and crunchy streusel on top (page 78).

Rose Pistachio Cake

This cake is really something special and a perfect introduction to this chapter. Almost everyone I know doubted this iconic Middle Eastern flavor combination when I first mentioned it, but after one bite, every one of them ended up mesmerized and wanting more. To bring the best possible, natural pistachio flavor to this recipe, I decided to use pistachio paste (see Note for how to make your own). Personally, I love adding cardamom to pistachios, but some might find it overpowering, even in small quantities, so it's listed here as an optional ingredient. The rose flavor comes in the form of a gorgeous and silky buttercream frosting. It's a strong flavor, so be careful with adding more than is listed, because you might get frosting that tastes soapy. And for the best possible taste, make sure to use real culinary rosewater.

- -

Serves 10 to 12

Pistachio Cake

Cooking spray or butter, for pans

2 cups (250 g) all-purpose flour

2 tsp (10 g) baking powder

¼ tsp ground cardamom (optional)

½ tsp fine sea salt (if your pistachio paste is unsalted)

¾ cup + 2 tbsp (210 g) sour cream, at room temperature

3 tbsp (45 ml) sunflower oil

½ tsp vanilla extract

½ cup (1 stick; 115 g) unsalted butter, at room temperature

½ cup (100 g) granulated sugar

⅔ cup (150 g) light brown sugar

4.5 oz (125 g) salted pistachio paste (see Note)

3 large eggs, at room temperature

Make the cake: Preheat the oven to 350°F (175°C) or 325°F (160°C) if using a fan-assisted oven. Grease three 6-inch (15-cm) round cake pans with cooking spray or butter and line the bottoms with parchment paper.

Sift the flour, baking powder, cardamom (if using) and salt (if using) into a medium-sized bowl and whisk to combine. In a measuring jug, lightly whisk together the sour cream, sunflower oil and vanilla.

Using a stand mixer fitted with the paddle attachment, beat the butter with the granulated sugar until pale and fluffy, 2 to 3 minutes. Add the brown sugar and the pistachio paste and beat to combine. Add the eggs, one at a time, making sure each is fully incorporated before adding the next.

Next, add the flour mixture in three additions, alternating with the sour cream mixture to avoid splashing and overmixing the batter. After each addition, mix the batter just until combined. Scrape the bowl a couple of times with a silicone spatula to make sure everything is mixed nicely.

Divide the batter equally by weight among the prepared pans and level it with an offset palette knife, then bake for 23 to 28 minutes. It's best to check the cakes after 23 minutes and then adjust the baking time accordingly, because ovens can vary. Your cakes are done when they're springy on the top and when a skewer inserted into the middle comes out mostly clean. When they're done, remove them from the oven and leave them to cool in their pans on a wire rack for 10 to 15 minutes to firm up a little bit before removing them from the pans to cool completely.

(continued)

Rosewater Buttercream

Scant ½ cup (55 g) all-purpose flour

1 cup + 1½ tbsp (220 g) granulated sugar

½ tsp fine sea salt

Scant 1⅔ cups (390 ml) whole milk

1½ cups + 2 tsp (3 sticks + 2 tsp; 350 g) unsalted butter, at room temperature

½ tsp vanilla extract

½ tsp rosewater

Rose/pink gel food coloring

Meanwhile, make the buttercream: In a small, heavy-bottomed saucepan, whisk together the flour, sugar, salt and milk. Cook over medium to high heat, whisking constantly so the mixture doesn't burn or catch in the bottom of the pan. Once it starts to thicken and you notice bubbling, cook for another 2 minutes, still whisking constantly, until it resembles pastry cream. This whole process could take up to 10 minutes.

When the pudding base is done, strain it through a sieve onto a shallow plate to get rid of any possible lumps. Cover it with plastic wrap touching the surface to prevent a skin from forming and let it cool to room temperature. You can speed up the process by letting it cool in the fridge, but prior to using, it must be room temperature.

Using the stand mixer fitted with the paddle attachment, beat the butter for 5 minutes, or until it's pale and fluffy. Then, add the previously made pudding base, one spoonful at a time. Beat everything until nicely incorporated with no lumps. Add the vanilla and rosewater, and beat until smooth and combined. Reserve 4 to 5 tablespoons (60 to 75 ml) of buttercream before proceeding to add little bit of rose gel food coloring into the rest of the buttercream, mixing until creamy and combined.

Assemble the cake: Start by leveling the tops of your cakes using a cake leveler or a long, serrated knife for a neater look, if needed. Then, put a little bit of buttercream in the middle of a serving plate or cake board to keep the cake from moving around. Place it on a turntable for easier handling and decorating.

Place one cake layer on the serving plate and, using a small, offset palette knife or a piping bag filled with buttercream, spread the frosting over the top of the cake layer, about ⅜ inch (1 cm) thick. Top it with the next cake layer and repeat the process. Place the final cake layer on top, making sure it's upside down to get a nice, smooth surface. Next, apply a thin layer of frosting around the cake and smooth it using a cake scraper to keep in the crumbs. Chill the cake in the fridge for 30 to 60 minutes before applying the final coat of frosting and decorating.

Once the crumb coat is firm, frost the cake with the remaining rose buttercream. Smooth the sides using a cake scraper, and the top using a small offset palette knife. Chill the cake for 30 to 60 minutes, or until firm. Take the cake from the fridge and dab some of the reserved white frosting on the sides of the cake using an offset palette knife. Gently smooth it using a cake scraper, for a textured effect.

Food-grade dried rose blossoms and pistachios for decorating (optional)

To decorate the top and sides of the cake, place the remaining buttercream (white, pink or both) into a piping bag fitted with an open star nozzle. Pipe rosettes and flowers in a curved shape and decorate with dried rose blossoms and pistachios.

Keep the cake tightly covered in plastic wrap or in an airtight container at room temperature for 2 days or in the fridge for up to a week. Allow it to come to room temperature before serving.

Note: You can make your own pistachio paste, as I do 99 percent of the time. In a food processor, pulse a scant 1¼ cups (150 g) of salted and roasted pistachios until the paste starts to look creamy and smooth. If you feel that the processing is taking too long and your food processor might be overheating, add 1 to 2 teaspoons (5 to 10 ml) of sunflower oil to help make it smooth and creamy in an instant. Do not add water under any circumstance, or the pistachio paste will split and won't be able to emulsify.

Honey *Lavender* Berry Cupcakes

The taste of these cupcakes will take you to a warm, sunny, late afternoon in the lavender fields of Provence—or at least that's what I imagine. I'm not really a big fan of honey's flavor—I can only drink it in tea—and I thought that lavender was only ever good in the back of my closet, but these cupcakes sure proved me wrong. The sweet honey and fragrant, herbaceous lavender pair beautifully in this recipe, creating a delicious, fluffy cupcake, topped with refreshing mixed-berry buttercream.

. . . .

Serves 12

Lavender-Infused Milk
⅔ cup (160 ml) whole milk

5 tbsp (15 g) dried culinary lavender

Berry Jam
17.5 oz (500 g) frozen mixed berries

¾ cup (150 g) sugar

Berry Buttercream
3⅓ tbsp (25 g) all-purpose flour

Scant ⅔ cup (120 g) sugar

Pinch of salt

Rounded ¾ cup (200 g) whole milk

13 tbsp (1½ sticks + 1 tbsp; 185 g) unsalted butter, at room temperature

3 to 4 tbsp (45 to 60 ml) berry jam

Make the lavender-infused milk: In a small saucepan, bring the milk to a simmer over medium-high heat. Once simmering, remove it from the stove, add the dried lavender, give it a stir, cover with a plate and let it steep for at least 20 to 30 minutes. Strain the milk through a fine-mesh sieve and measure out the scant ½ cup (120 ml) that will be needed for the cupcakes. Set aside until needed.

Make the berry jam: In a small saucepan, combine the berries and sugar. Bring to a simmer over medium-high heat, stirring occasionally so the mixture doesn't catch on the bottom of the pan. Press the berries with the back of a silicone spatula or a wooden spoon to speed up the process. Simmer until the mixture is thick, 15 to 20 minutes.

Remove from the heat, strain through a sieve onto a small plate or puree with an immersion blender, then cover with plastic wrap touching the surface to prevent a skin forming and let cool completely before using.

Begin the buttercream: In a small, heavy-bottomed saucepan, whisk together the flour, sugar, salt and milk. Cook over medium to high heat, whisking constantly so the mixture doesn't burn or catch on the bottom of the pan. Once it starts to thicken and you notice bubbling, cook for another 2 minutes, still whisking continuously, until it resembles pastry cream. This whole process could take up to 10 minutes.

When the pudding base is done, strain it through a sieve onto a shallow plate to get rid of any lumps. Cover it with plastic wrap touching the surface to prevent a skin from forming and let it cool to room temperature. You can speed up the process by letting it cool in the fridge, but prior to using, it must be room temperature.

(continued)

Honey *Lavender* Berry Cupcakes (Continued)

Honey Lavender Cupcakes

1⅔ cups (200 g) all-purpose flour

1½ tsp (7.5 g) baking powder

¼ tsp baking soda

½ tsp fine sea salt

2 large eggs, at room temperature

½ cup (100 g) sugar

6⅔ tbsp (100 ml) sunflower oil

¼ cup (60 ml) honey

Scant ½ cup (120 g) lavender milk

Make the cupcakes: Preheat the oven to 350°F (175°C) or 325°F (160°C) if using a fan-assisted oven. Line a cupcake pan with 12 paper liners.

Sift the flour, baking powder, baking soda and salt into a medium-sized bowl and whisk to combine. Using a stand mixer fitted with the whisk attachment, or medium-sized bowl and an electric hand mixer, beat the eggs with the sugar until doubled in size, pale and fluffy. Add the sunflower oil and honey and beat on low speed until combined. Add the flour mixture and beat until just combined. Pour in the reserved lavender milk and beat for a few seconds until you get a smooth but liquid batter. Scrape the bowl with a silicone spatula to ensure everything is fully incorporated.

Fill the prepared paper liners three-quarters of the way full and bake for 18 to 20 minutes. The cupcakes are done if they spring back when lightly touched. Remove from the oven and let them firm up in the pan for 3 to 4 minutes before transferring them to a wire rack to cool completely.

Meanwhile, finish the buttercream: Using the stand mixer fitted with the paddle attachment, beat the butter for 5 minutes, or until it's pale and fluffy. Then, add spoonful by spoonful of the previously made pudding. Beat everything until it's all nicely incorporated with no lumps. Add the berry jam and mix until smooth and combined.

Assemble the cupcakes: Make a hole in the center of each cupcake using an apple corer, and fill with berry puree. Transfer the buttercream to a piping bag fitted with an open star nozzle and make rosettes on top of the cupcakes.

The cupcakes are best when served the same day at room temperature, but you can keep them in an airtight container at room temperature for 2 days. Any longer and they will dry out substantially.

Strawberry *Elderflower* Cake

Elderflower syrup is one of those things that people across my country make from scratch when spring arrives. I hadn't thought about using it in a cake, until the famous Meghan and Harry royal wedding took place. So, this cake is inspired by their lemon elderflower wedding cake, only I opted for delicious strawberry frosting—because even royals can't say no to strawberries!

. . . .

Serves 12 to 14

Strawberry Jam

17.5 oz (500 g) fresh or frozen strawberries

¾ cup (150 g) granulated sugar

1 tbsp (15 ml) fresh lemon juice

Strawberry Buttercream

¼ cup + 2 tbsp (45 g) all-purpose flour

1 cup (200 g) sugar

¼ tsp fine sea salt

1½ cups (360 ml) whole milk

1⅓ cups (2⅔ sticks; 300 g) unsalted butter, at room temperature

1 tsp vanilla extract

5 to 6 tbsp (75 to 90 ml) strawberry jam

Elderflower Cake

Cooking spray or butter, for pans

2 cups (250 g) all-purpose flour

2 tsp (10 g) baking powder

½ tsp fine sea salt

¼ cup + 2 tsp (80 g) elderflower cordial

Rounded ¾ cup (180 g) sour cream, at room temperature

2 tbsp (30 ml) whole milk, at room temperature

3 tbsp (45 ml) sunflower oil

2 tbsp (30 ml) fresh lemon juice

Finely grated zest of 1 lemon

½ tsp vanilla extract

½ cup (1 stick; 115 g) unsalted butter, at room temperature

Rounded cup (220 g) granulated sugar

3 large eggs, at room temperature

Make the strawberry jam: In a small saucepan, bring the strawberries and sugar to a simmer over medium-high heat, stirring occasionally so the mixture doesn't catch on the bottom of the pan. Press the strawberries with the back of the silicone spatula or a wooden spoon to speed up the process. Simmer until the mixture is thick, 15 to 20 minutes.

Remove from the heat, add the lemon juice and puree with an immersion blender until smooth. Transfer the jam to a jar and place in the fridge to cool completely.

Begin the buttercream: In a small, heavy-bottomed saucepan, whisk together the flour, sugar, salt and milk. Cook over medium to high heat, whisking constantly so the mixture doesn't burn or catch on the bottom of the pan. Once it starts to thicken and you notice bubbling, cook for another 2 minutes, still whisking constantly, until it resembles pastry cream. This could take about 10 minutes.

When the pudding base is done, strain it through a sieve onto a shallow plate to get rid of any lumps. Cover it with plastic wrap touching the surface to prevent a skin from forming and let it cool to room temperature. You can speed up the process by letting it cool in the fridge, but prior to using, it must be room temperature.

Make the cake: Preheat the oven to 350°F (175°C) or 325°F (160°C) if using a fan-assisted oven. Grease three 6-inch (15-cm) round cake pans with cooking spray or butter and line the bottoms with parchment paper.

Sift the flour, baking powder and salt into a medium-sized bowl and whisk to combine. In a measuring jug, lightly whisk together the elderflower cordial, sour cream, milk, sunflower oil, lemon juice, lemon zest and vanilla.

(continued)

Using a stand mixer fitted with the paddle attachment, beat the butter with half of the sugar until pale and fluffy, 2 to 3 minutes. Add the rest of the sugar and beat to combine. Add the eggs, one at a time, making sure each is fully incorporated before adding the next.

Next, add the flour mixture in three additions, alternating with the sour cream mixture to avoid splashing and overmixing the batter. After each addition, mix the batter just until combined. Scrape the bowl a couple of times with a silicone spatula to make sure everything is mixed nicely.

Divide the batter equally by weight among the prepared pans and level it with an offset palette knife, then bake for 22 to 25 minutes. It's best to check the cakes after 22 minutes and then adjust the baking time accordingly, because ovens can vary. The cakes are done if they spring back when lightly touched and when a skewer inserted into the middle comes out mostly clean. Remove them from the oven and leave them to cool in their pans on a wire rack for 10 to 15 minutes to firm up a little bit before removing them from the pans to cool completely.

While the cakes are cooling, finish the buttercream: Using the stand mixer fitted with the paddle attachment, beat the butter for 5 minutes, or until it's pale and fluffy. Then, add the previously made pudding one spoonful at a time. Beat everything until nicely incorporated with no lumps. Lastly, add the vanilla and the strawberry jam and beat until smooth and combined.

Assemble the cake: Start by leveling the tops of your cakes using a cake leveler or a long, serrated knife for a neater look, if needed. Then, put a little bit of buttercream in the middle of a serving plate or your cake board to keep the cake from moving around. Place it on a turntable for easier handling and decorating.

Place one cake layer on the serving plate and, using a small, offset palette knife or a piping bag filled with buttercream, spread the frosting over the top of the cake, about ⅜ inch (1 cm) thick. Make a dam around the edges and fill with a couple of tablespoons (about 30 ml) of strawberry jam. Top it with the next cake layer and repeat the process. Place the final cake layer on top, making sure it's upside down to get a nice, smooth surface.

Next, apply a thin layer of frosting around the cake and smooth it using a cake scraper to keep in the crumbs. Chill the cake in the fridge for 30 to 60 minutes before applying the final coat of frosting and decorating.

Once the crumb coat is firm, frost the cake with the remaining buttercream. Smooth the sides using a cake scraper, and the top using a small offset palette knife. Put the buttercream into a piping bag fitted with a French star nozzle and pipe dollops on top.

Keep the cake tightly covered in plastic wrap or in an airtight container at room temperature for 2 days or in the fridge for up to a week. Allow it to come to room temperature before serving.

Earl Grey Blackberry White Chocolate Cake

I wasn't much of a tea drinker up until my early twenties. One could say I didn't really cherish the existence of tea; it was mostly used only as a cough remedy. But then something hit me—truthfully, it might have been *Downton Abbey*—and I discovered a whole new world. Earl Grey tea, with its lovely bergamot notes, rapidly became one of my favorite flavors. Making it into a cake was only a matter of time, and it's now one of the most popular recipes on my blog, as well as in my family. Here I've paired it with a sweet but tart blackberry filling and a creamy white chocolate frosting, which complement each other fantastically.

. . . .

Serves 12 to 14

Blackberry Jam

12 oz (350 g) fresh or frozen blackberries (see Note)

Scant ⅔ cup (125 g) granulated sugar

Zest of 1 orange

Earl Grey–Infused Milk

1 cup + 2 tsp (250 ml) whole milk

2½ tbsp (15 g) loose-leaf Earl Grey tea

White Chocolate Buttercream

⅓ cup (40 g) all-purpose flour

⅔ cup (130 g) granulated sugar

¼ tsp fine sea salt

1½ cups (360 ml) whole milk

5.5 oz (150 g) white chocolate, finely chopped

1⅓ cups (2⅔ sticks; 300 g) unsalted butter, at room temperature

1½ tsp (8 ml) vanilla extract

Burgundy gel food coloring (optional)

Make the blackberry jam: In a small saucepan, bring the blackberries, sugar and orange zest to a simmer over medium-high heat, stirring occasionally so the mixture doesn't catch on the bottom of the pan. Simmer until the mixture is thick and gloopy, 15 to 20 minutes. Remove from the heat and strain through a sieve to get rid of the seeds. Stir to combine, then transfer to a jar. Place in the fridge to cool completely until needed.

Make the Earl Grey–infused milk: In a small saucepan, bring the milk to a simmer. Remove from the heat and add the tea leaves, give it a stir, cover with a plate and let steep for at least 20 to 30 minutes. Strain the milk through a fine-mesh sieve and measure out the ¾ cup (180 ml) needed for the cake. Set this aside until needed.

Begin the buttercream: In a small, heavy-bottomed saucepan, whisk together the flour, sugar, salt and milk. Cook over medium to high heat, whisking constantly so the mixture doesn't burn or catch on the bottom of the pan. Once it starts to thicken and you notice bubbling, cook for another 2 minutes, still whisking constantly, until it resembles pastry cream. This whole process could take about 10 minutes.

When the pudding base is done, strain it through a sieve onto a shallow plate to get rid of any lumps. Cover it with plastic wrap touching the surface to prevent a skin from forming and let it cool to room temperature. You can speed up the process by letting it cool in the fridge, but prior to using, it must be room temperature.

(continued)

Earl Grey Blackberry White Chocolate Cake
(Continued)

. . . .

Earl Grey Cake

Cooking spray or butter, for pans

2 cups (250 g) all-purpose flour

2 tsp (10 g) baking powder

½ tsp fine sea salt

¾ cup (180 g) Earl Grey–infused milk, room temperature

¼ cup (60 g) sour cream, at room temperature

3 tbsp (45 ml) sunflower oil

½ tsp vanilla extract

⅔ cup (1⅓ sticks; 150 g) unsalted butter, at room temperature

1¼ cups (250 g) granulated sugar

3 large eggs, at room temperature

Make the cake: Preheat the oven to 350°F (175°C) or 325°F (160°C) if using a fan-assisted oven. Grease three 6-inch (15-cm) round cake pans with cooking spray or butter and line the bottoms with parchment paper.

Sift the flour, baking powder and salt into a medium-sized bowl and whisk to combine. In a measuring jug, lightly whisk together the Earl Grey–infused milk, sour cream, sunflower oil and vanilla. Using a stand mixer fitted with the paddle attachment, beat the butter with half of the sugar until pale and fluffy, 2 to 3 minutes. Add the rest of the sugar and beat to combine. Add the eggs, one at a time, making sure each is fully incorporated before adding the next.

Next, add the flour mixture in three additions, alternating with the sour cream mixture to avoid splashing and overmixing the batter. After each addition, mix the batter just until combined. Scrape the bowl a couple of times with a silicone spatula to make sure everything is mixed nicely.

Divide the batter equally by weight among the prepared pans and level it with an offset palette knife, then bake for 22 to 25 minutes. It's best to check the cakes after 22 minutes and then adjust the baking time accordingly, because ovens can vary. The cakes are done when they're springy on the top and when a skewer inserted into the middle comes out mostly clean. Remove the cakes from the oven and leave them to cool in their pans on a wire rack for 10 to 15 minutes to firm up a little bit before inverting them onto a wire rack to cool completely.

While the cakes are cooling, finish the buttercream: Melt the white chocolate in a small, heatproof bowl placed over a pan of simmering water. Set aside to slightly cool.

Using the stand mixer fitted with the paddle attachment, beat the butter for 5 minutes, or until it's pale and fluffy, then add the previously made pudding base, one spoonful at a time. Beat everything until nicely incorporated with no lumps. Lastly, add the vanilla and the melted chocolate and beat until smooth and combined.

Fresh or freeze-dried
blackberries, for decoration
(optional)

Assemble the cake: Start by leveling the tops of your cakes using a cake leveler or a long, serrated knife for a neater look, if needed. Then, put a little bit of buttercream in the middle of a serving plate or cake board to keep the cake from moving around. Place it on a turntable for easier handling and decorating.

Place one cake layer on the serving plate and using a small, offset palette knife or a piping bag filled with buttercream, spread the frosting over the top of the cake, about ⅜ inch (1 cm) thick. Make a dam around it and fill with a couple of tablespoons (about 30 ml) of blackberry jam. Top it with the next cake layer and repeat the process. Place the final cake layer on top, making sure it's upside down to get a nice, smooth surface on top.

Next, apply a thin layer of frosting around the cake and smooth it using a cake scraper to keep in the crumbs. Chill the cake in the fridge for 30 to 60 minutes before applying the final coat of frosting and decorating.

Once the crumb coat is firm, frost the cake with the remaining buttercream, saving some for the decorative brush strokes on the lower sides of the cake. Smooth the sides and the top using a cake scraper and a small offset palette knife. Chill the cake for an additional 30 minutes before adding the finishing touches.

Tint the leftover buttercream with some burgundy gel food coloring in three shades and make brush strokes with an offset palette knife, starting on the bottom side of the cake. Top the cake with buttercream rosettes and/or blackberries, if desired.

Keep the cake tightly covered in plastic wrap or in an airtight container at room temperature for 2 days or in the fridge for up to a week. Allow it it to come to room temperature before serving.

Note: If using fresh blackberries to make the jam, add a couple of tablespoons (about 30 ml) of water to the pan to help dissolve the sugar.

Raspberry **Rose Loaf Cake**

Raspberries and rose go hand in hand beautifully, and this cake is here to prove it to you. Although some might think of rose as too perfumelike or soapy a flavor, when done right, its floral notes complement the sharp raspberries in the most sophisticated way. The special loaf tin is what gives this dessert its luxurious appearance, so this cake turns out to be a delicious stunner with as little effort as possible.

· ·

Serves 10 to 12

Cake
Cooking spray or butter, for pan

Scant 1½ cups (180 g) all-purpose flour

1½ tsp (7.5 g) baking powder

¾ cup + 2 tbsp (175 g) granulated sugar

¼ tsp fine sea salt

⅔ cup (150 g) sour cream, at room temperature

¼ cup (60 ml) sunflower oil

2 large eggs, at room temperature

1 tsp rosewater

¼ cup (½ stick; 55 g) unsalted butter, at room temperature

5.5 oz (150 g) fresh raspberries, plus more for decorating

Glaze
Rounded ¾ cup (100 g) powdered sugar, or as needed

1 to 3 tbsp (15 to 45 ml) whole milk

1 tsp rosewater

Make the cake: Preheat the oven to 350°F (175°C) or 325°F (160°C) if using a fan-assisted oven. Grease a 6-cup (1.5-L) loaf pan with cooking spray or butter.

Sift the flour, baking powder, sugar and salt into the bowl of a stand mixer, or a medium-sized bowl if you're using an electric hand mixer, and whisk to combine.

In a measuring jug, lightly whisk together the sour cream, sunflower oil, eggs and rosewater. Add the butter to the flour mixture, fit the stand mixer with the paddle attachment and mix on low speed until you get a sandlike texture and there are no traces of flour.

Next, add the sour cream mixture in two equal batches to avoid splashing and overmixing the batter. After each addition, mix the batter for about 15 seconds, or until everything is fully incorporated. Scrape the bowl a couple of times with a silicone spatula to make sure everything is mixed nicely. Fold in the raspberries.

Scrape the batter into the prepared pan and level it with an offset palette knife. Bake for 40 to 45 minutes. The cake is done if it springs back when lightly touched or when a skewer inserted into the middle comes out mostly clean. Remove the cake from the oven and allow it to cool in the pan for 10 minutes to firm up before carefully inverting onto a wire rack to cool completely.

Make the glaze: In a small bowl, whisk together the sugar, milk and rosewater. For a thicker glaze, add less milk and more sugar; for a thinner glaze, add more milk and less sugar.

To serve, pour the glaze over the cooled cake and top with fresh raspberries.

Keep the cake tightly covered in plastic wrap or in an airtight container at room temperature for 2 days or in the fridge for up to a week. Allow it to come to room temperature before serving.

> **Note:** This recipe can also be made in a 9-inch (23-cm) round pan or a 9 x 5-inch (23 x 13-cm) loaf pan, but will turn out shorter. Depending on which pan you choose, the baking time will vary, so keep an eye on it.

Orange Blossom **Ricotta Bundt Cake**

Baking Bundt cakes always gives me such satisfaction, because you get a beautiful-looking cake with very little effort. Take this gorgeous cake, for example. The combination of ricotta and buttermilk make the cake wonderfully tender and moist, where each slice is full of fragrant yet slightly bittersweet orange blossom flavor. And the best part is that it comes together in less than 90 minutes! It's a great choice with a cup of tea, and it stays moist for days.

. . . .

Serves 12 to 14

Cake
Cooking spray or butter, for pan

Scant 2½ cups (300 g)
all-purpose flour

2½ tsp (12.5 g) baking powder

¼ tsp baking soda

½ tsp fine sea salt

1 cup (250 g) ricotta cheese,
at room temperature

¾ cup (180 ml) sunflower oil

1¾ cups (350 g) granulated sugar

3 large eggs, at room
temperature

2 tsp (10 ml) orange blossom
water

¾ cup (180 ml) buttermilk, at
room temperature

Preheat the oven to 350°F (175°C) or 325°F (160°C) if using a fan-assisted oven. Grease a 10-cup (2.4-L) Bundt pan with cooking spray or butter.

Sift the flour, baking powder, baking soda and salt into a large bowl and whisk to combine. In a separate large bowl, using an electric hand mixer, beat the ricotta cheese and sunflower oil with the sugar, until creamy and combined. Add the eggs, one at a time, making sure each is fully incorporated before adding the next. Add the orange blossom water and beat to combine.

Next, add the flour mixture to the ricotta mixture in three batches, alternating with the buttermilk. After each addition, beat the batter just until incorporated. Scrape the bowl a couple of times with a silicone spatula to make sure everything is mixed nicely.

Scrape the batter into the prepared pan and bake for 45 to 50 minutes, or until a skewer inserted into the middle comes out mostly clean. It's best to check the cake after 40 minutes and then adjust the baking time accordingly, because ovens can vary.

When the cake is done, remove it from the oven and allow to cool in the pan for 15 minutes before carefully inverting it onto a wire rack to cool completely.

Store the cake in an airtight container at room temperature for 3 to 4 days or up to a week in the fridge.

Note: If you'd like a simple sugar glaze on top, see the directions for the glaze (leaving out the rosewater) in the Raspberry Rose Loaf Cake (page 66).

Jasmine **Green Tea Vanilla Cake**

My obsession with making tea-infused cakes is real and on full display in this recipe. The simple, moist vanilla cake lets the sweet, floral jasmine really shine through the buttercream, without being overpowering. To infuse the milk with jasmine flavor, I used loose-leaf tea, but you can also use tea bags of your favorite brand in the same quantity (I recommend Ahmad tea). If you're a tea lover who is looking to try something new, I would start with this incredible recipe!

· ·

Serves 12 to 14

Jasmine Tea–Infused Milk
Scant 2 cups (460 ml) whole milk

Scant 4 tbsp (20 g) loose-leaf jasmine green tea

Jasmine Buttercream
Rounded ¼ cup (45 g) all-purpose flour

1 cup (200 g) granulated sugar

¼ tsp fine sea salt

1½ cups (360 ml) jasmine tea–infused milk

1⅓ cups (2⅔ sticks; 300 g) unsalted butter, at room temperature

½ tsp vanilla extract

Vanilla Cake
Cooking spray or butter, for pans

2 cups (250 g) all-purpose flour

2 tsp (10 g) baking powder

½ tsp fine sea salt

Rounded ¾ cup (180 g) sour cream, at room temperature

¼ cup (60 ml) whole milk, at room temperature

3 tbsp (45 ml) sunflower oil

2 tsp (10 ml) vanilla extract

½ cup (1 stick; 115 g) unsalted butter, at room temperature

1¼ cups (250 g) granulated sugar

3 large eggs, at room temperature

Make the jasmine tea–infused milk: In a small saucepan, bring the milk to a simmer over medium-high heat. Remove from the heat, add the jasmine tea and give it a stir. Cover with a plate and let steep for at least 20 to 30 minutes. Strain it through a sieve and set aside 1½ cups (360 ml) until needed for the buttercream.

Begin the buttercream: In a small, heavy-bottomed saucepan, whisk together the flour, sugar, salt and jasmine tea–infused milk. Cook over medium to high heat, whisking constantly so the mixture doesn't burn or catch on the bottom of the pan. Once it starts to thicken and you notice bubbling, cook for another 2 minutes, still whisking constantly, until it resembles pastry cream. This whole process could take up to 10 minutes.

When the pudding base is done, strain it through a sieve onto a shallow plate to get rid of any lumps. Cover it with plastic wrap touching the surface to prevent a skin from forming and let it cool to room temperature. You can speed up the process by letting it cool in the fridge, but prior to using, it must be room temperature.

Make the cake: Preheat the oven to 350°F (175°C) or 325°F (160°C) if using a fan-assisted oven. Grease three 6-inch (15-cm) round cake pans with cooking spray or butter and line the bottoms with parchment paper.

Sift the flour, baking powder and salt into a medium-sized bowl and whisk to combine. In a measuring jug, lightly whisk together the sour cream, milk, sunflower oil and vanilla.

Using a stand mixer fitted with the paddle attachment, beat the butter with half of the sugar until pale and fluffy, 2 to 3 minutes. Add the rest of the sugar and beat to combine. Add the eggs, one at a time, making sure each is fully incorporated before adding the next.

Next, add the flour mixture in three additions, alternating with the sour cream mixture to avoid splashing and overmixing the batter. After each addition, mix the batter just until combined. Scrape the bowl a couple of times with a silicone spatula to make sure everything is mixed nicely.

(continued)

Edible flowers, for decoration (optional)

Divide the batter equally by weight among the prepared pans and level it with an offset palette knife, then bake for 22 to 25 minutes. It's best to check the cakes after 22 minutes and then adjust the baking time accordingly, because ovens can vary. The cakes are done when they're springy on the top and when a skewer inserted into the middle comes out mostly clean. When they're done, remove them from the oven and leave them to cool in their pans on a wire rack for 10 to 15 minutes to firm up a little bit before removing them from the pans to cool completely.

While the cakes are cooling, finish the buttercream: Using the stand mixer fitted with the paddle attachment, beat the butter for at least 5 minutes, or until it's pale and fluffy, then add the previously made pudding base, one spoonful at a time. Beat everything until nicely incorporated with no lumps. Add the vanilla and beat for a couple of seconds, until smooth and combined.

Assemble the cake: Start by leveling the tops of your cakes using a cake leveler or a long, serrated knife for a neater look, if needed. Then, put a little bit of buttercream in the middle of a serving plate or cake board to keep the cake from moving around. Place it on a turntable for easier handling and decorating.

Place one cake layer on the serving plate and, using a small, offset palette knife or a piping bag filled with buttercream, spread the frosting over the top of the cake layer, about ⅜ inch (1 cm) thick. Top it with the next cake layer and repeat the process. Place the final cake layer on top, making sure it's upside down to get a nice, smooth surface on top.

Next, apply a thin layer of frosting around the cake and smooth it using a cake scraper to keep in the crumbs. Chill the cake in the fridge for 30 to 60 minutes before applying the final coat of frosting and decorating.

Once the crumb coat is firm, place the cake on the turntable, frost with the remaining buttercream and smooth the sides and the top using a cake scraper. Pipe some rosettes across the top and the sides of the cake in a curved line and decorate with edible flowers, if desired.

Note: For a little bit of a tang and freshness, try filling the cake with raspberry jam (page 73); it pairs beautifully with jasmine and vanilla.

Raspberry **White Chocolate Cake**

I don't know if you can tell, but raspberries are probably my favorite berry. In this incredible cake, their delicate, fresh, tangy flavor works wonderfully with the sweet white chocolate. The addition of white chocolate in the cake batter gives it a creamy, milky flavor and a moist, dense texture that I just love. For an extra cute look, I topped the cake with meringue kisses, which is my favorite way of decorating.

. . . .

Serves 12 to 14

Raspberry Jam
17.5 oz (500 g) fresh or frozen raspberries, plus more for decorating

¾ cup (150 g) granulated sugar

1 tbsp (15 g) fresh lemon juice

White Chocolate Raspberry Buttercream
⅓ cup (40 g) all-purpose flour

Scant ⅔ cup (130 g) granulated sugar

¼ tsp fine sea salt

1½ cups (360 ml) whole milk

1⅓ cups (2⅔ sticks; 300 g) unsalted butter, at room temperature

3.5 oz (100 g) white chocolate, melted

3 to 4 tbsp (45 to 60 ml) raspberry jam

Pink gel food coloring

Make the raspberry jam: In a small saucepan, bring the raspberries and sugar to a simmer over medium-high heat, stirring occasionally so the mixture doesn't catch on the bottom of the pan. Simmer until it is thick and gloopy, 15 to 20 minutes.

Remove from the heat and strain through a sieve to get rid of the seeds. Add the lemon juice, stir to combine and transfer to a jar. Place the jam in the fridge to cool completely until needed.

Begin the buttercream: In a small, heavy-bottomed saucepan whisk together the flour, sugar, salt and milk. Cook over medium to high heat, whisking constantly so the mixture doesn't burn or catch on the bottom of the pan. Once it starts to thicken and you notice bubbling, cook for another 2 minutes, still whisking constantly, until it resembles pastry cream. This whole process could take about 10 minutes.

When the pudding base is done, strain it through a sieve onto a shallow plate to get rid of any lumps. Cover it with plastic wrap touching the surface to prevent a skin from forming and let it cool to room temperature. You can speed up the process by letting it cool in the fridge, but prior to using, it must be room temperature.

(continued)

White Chocolate Cake

Cooking spray or butter, for pans

4.5 oz (125 g) white chocolate, at least 28%, finely chopped

⅔ cup (160 ml) whole milk, at room temperature

2 cups (250 g) all-purpose flour

2¼ tsp (12 g) baking powder

½ tsp fine sea salt

Rounded ½ cup (120 g) sour cream, at room temperature

3 tbsp (45 ml) sunflower oil

1 tsp vanilla extract

½ cup (1 stick; 115 g) unsalted butter, at room temperature

1 cup (200 g) granulated sugar

3 large eggs, at room temperature

Make the cake: Preheat the oven to 350°F (175°C) or 325°F (160°C) if using a fan-assisted oven. Grease three 6-inch (15-cm) round cake pans with cooking spray or butter and line the bottoms with parchment paper.

In a small, heavy-bottomed saucepan, melt the white chocolate and milk together over medium-high heat, whisking occasionally, until combined. Set aside to cool to room temperature until needed.

Sift the flour, baking powder and salt into a large bowl and whisk together. In a measuring jug, lightly whisk together the white chocolate mixture, sour cream, sunflower oil and vanilla.

Using a stand mixer fitted with the paddle attachment, beat the butter with half of the sugar until pale and fluffy, 2 to 3 minutes. Add the rest of the sugar and beat to combine. Add the eggs, one at a time, making sure each is fully incorporated before adding the next.

Next, add the flour mixture in three additions, alternating with the sour cream mixture to avoid splashing and overmixing the batter. After each addition, mix the batter just until combined. Scrape the bowl a couple of times with a silicone spatula to make sure everything is getting mixed nicely.

Divide the batter equally by weight among the prepared pans and level it with an offset palette knife. Bake for 22 to 25 minutes. It's best to check the cakes after 22 minutes and then adjust the baking time accordingly, because ovens can vary. The cakes are done if they spring back when lightly touched and when a skewer inserted into the middle comes out mostly clean. Remove from the oven and leave them to cool in their pans on a wire rack for 10 to 15 minutes to firm up a little bit before removing them from the pans to cool completely.

(continued)

Meringue Kisses

3 oz (80 g) fresh egg whites (about 2 large eggs)

Rounded ¾ cup (160 g) granulated sugar

½ tsp salt

Make the meringue kisses: Clean the bowl of your stand mixer, as well as the whisk attachment, using a little bit of lemon juice or vinegar and a clean paper towel. This way you're eliminating any traces of fat that could make making meringue impossible.

In the clean bowl, combine the egg whites, sugar and salt and place over a pot of simmering water. Make sure the bowl doesn't touch the water. Stir constantly with a whisk to make sure the egg whites cook evenly. The mixture is done when it's hot and the sugar is completely dissolved, 2 to 4 minutes. Rub a little bit of the mixture between your fingers to test. If you can feel the sugar granules, cook the egg whites some more, stirring constantly.

Ideally, the mixture should reach 160°F (70°C). But if you don't have a thermometer, just make sure it's hot and smooth.

Wipe the outside surface of the bowl, place it on your stand mixer, fit the mixer with the whisk attachment and mix the egg whites on high speed until your meringue reaches stiff peaks and the sides of the bowl are cool to the touch. This could take anywhere from 5 to 15 minutes.

Meanwhile, preheat your oven to 210°F (100°C) and line a baking sheet with parchment paper. Use some prepared meringue to stick the paper to the pan so it won't slide and move while you're piping.

Put the meringue into a large piping bag fitted with French open star nozzle or a large round nozzle. Holding your piping bag vertically, pipe meringue kisses in equal rows across the paper. Bake them for 40 to 45 minutes, or until you can pick them up without them sticking to the paper. Store in an airtight container.

While the cakes are cooling, finish the buttercream: Using the stand mixer fitted with the paddle attachment, beat the butter for 5 minutes, or until it's pale and fluffy, then add the previously made pudding base, one spoonful at a time. Beat everything until nicely incorporated with no lumps. Lastly, add the melted white chocolate and beat until smooth and combined.

Divide the buttercream into two equal portions, leaving one of them in the bowl of the stand mixer. Add the raspberry jam to the portion in the bowl and beat until smooth and combined (reserve the rest of the jam for assembly).

White Chocolate Ganache

2 oz (60 g) white chocolate, finely chopped

3 tbsp (45 g) heavy cream

White gel food coloring

Assemble the cake: Start by leveling the tops of your cakes using a cake leveler or a long, serrated knife for a neater look, if needed. Then, put a little bit of buttercream in the middle of a serving plate or your cake board to keep the cake from moving around. Place it on a turntable for easier handling and decorating.

Place one cake layer on the serving plate and, using a small, offset palette knife or a piping bag, spread the raspberry frosting over the top of the cake layer, about ⅜ inch (1 cm) thick. Make a dam around it and fill with some raspberry jam. Top it with the next cake layer and repeat the process. Place the final cake layer on top, making sure it's upside down to get a nice, smooth surface on top.

Next, apply a thin layer of raspberry frosting around the cake and smooth it using a cake scraper to keep in the crumbs. Chill the cake in the fridge for 30 to 60 minutes before applying the final coat of frosting and decorating.

Once the crumb coat is firm, frost the cake with the remaining (jam-free) white chocolate buttercream. Smooth the sides using a cake scraper, and the top using a small offset palette knife. Chill the cake for 30 to 60 minutes, or until firm. In the meantime, tint the leftover buttercream into two to three different shades of pink using gel food coloring. Take the cake from the fridge and dab some of the pink frosting on the sides of the cake using an offset palette knife. Gently smooth it using a cake scraper for a textured watercolor effect.

Make the white chocolate ganache: Combine the white chocolate and cream in a small, heatproof bowl and melt together over a small pot of simmering water. Alternatively, you can do this (using a microwave- safe bowl) in a microwave in 30-second intervals. Add some white food coloring, mix well with a small silicone spatula and leave for 10 to 15 minutes to thicken a little bit before pouring over the chilled cake. Pour two-thirds of the white chocolate ganache onto the middle of your cake and slowly spread it around with a small offset palette knife for a natural-looking drip. If you need more, add the remaining third of the ganache on top and spread it in the same manner. The final quantity needed depends on how thick the ganache is and how chilled the cake is.

Top the cake with meringue kisses, any leftover buttercream and fresh raspberries.

Keep the cake tightly covered at room temperature for 2 days or up to a week in the fridge. Allow it to come to room temperature before serving.

Blueberry **Streusel Lemon Cheesecake**

My family and I are big cheesecake lovers. The main reason I perfected the recipe so early in my baking journey is that at one point, I'd been making this cheesecake every week. This version is slightly modified to support the topping, but is just as creamy as the original. The gooey blueberry pie filling and the crunchy streusel topping only take it to the next level. I like to add a little cardamom to the blueberries, but feel free to omit that or use a little bit of cinnamon instead.

Serves 12 to 14

Streusel
Scant ¾ cup (90 g) all-purpose flour

¼ tsp fine sea salt

3 tbsp + 1 tsp (50 g) soft light brown sugar

¼ cup + 1 tsp (½ stick + 1 tsp; 60 g) unsalted butter, melted

1 tbsp (5 g) rolled oats

Blueberry Pie Filling
10 oz (280 g) fresh or frozen blueberries

Scant ⅓ cup (70 g) soft light brown sugar

¼ tsp ground cardamom (optional)

1 tbsp (15 ml) fresh lemon juice

Rounded tbsp (10 g) cornstarch + 1 to 2 tbsp (15 to 30 ml) water

Crust
Cooking spray or butter, for pan

9 oz (250 g) graham crackers or digestive biscuits

1 tbsp (15 g) soft light brown sugar

¼ tsp ground cinnamon

½ cup + 2 tsp (1 stick + 2 tsp; 125 g) unsalted butter, melted

Cheesecake Filling
24 oz (680 g) full-fat cream cheese, at room temperature

¾ cup (150 g) granulated sugar

Finely grated zest and juice of 2 lemons (you need about ¼ cup [70 g] of juice)

4 large eggs, at room temperature

Make the streusel: Sift and combine the flour, salt and brown sugar into a small bowl. Gradually add the melted butter while stirring with a fork, until the mixture starts clumping together. Add the rolled oats, stir to combine and put in the fridge until needed.

Make the blueberry pie filling: In a small saucepan, combine the blueberries, brown sugar, cardamom (if using) and lemon juice and bring to a boil over medium heat. Simmer for a few minutes.

In a small bowl, dilute the cornstarch with the water and pour the mixture over the blueberries, stirring constantly with a large wooden spoon until everything is incorporated. Bring the mixture to a boil and cook for a few minutes, or until gloopy and thick. If the filling is too thick, you can always add some more water, but keep in mind the filling will thicken additionally once completely cooled. Once thickened, transfer the mixture to a bowl and cover with plastic wrap touching the surface to prevent a skin from forming. Put it in the fridge to cool completely.

Make the crust: Preheat the oven to 350°F (175°C) or 325°F (160°C) if using a fan-assisted oven. Lightly grease a 9-inch (23-cm) round springform pan with cooking spray or butter and line the base with parchment paper.

In a food processor, pulse the graham crackers until finely ground. Add the brown sugar, cinnamon and melted butter and pulse until evenly combined. Transfer the mixture to the prepared pan and press firmly to create an even layer, pressing a little up the sides of the pan as well. Bake for 7 to 8 minutes, then remove from the oven and set aside.

Make the cheesecake filling: In a large bowl, combine the cream cheese, sugar, lemon zest and juice, and beat using an electric hand mixer, until smooth. Add the eggs, one at a time, making sure each is fully incorporated before adding the next. Scrape the bowl a couple of times with a silicone spatula to make sure everything is mixed nicely.

Pour the filling over the crust and spread into an even layer. Gently dollop the blueberry pie filling on top and sprinkle with streusel. Bake for 30 to 35 minutes, or until the cheesecake is set around the edges with a little wobble in the middle. Remove from the oven and leave in the pan on a wire rack to cool to room temperature before putting in the fridge to cool completely—at least 4 hours before serving.

Chamomile Apple Cake

Similar to honey, I'm not a big fan of chamomile tea, but I love the scent of it in the hand creams my grandmother always uses. Its earthy, floral tones also pair wonderfully with apples, giving you a light, weekend afternoon dessert—preferably with a movie involved. My favorite apples are either Pink Lady (also known as Cripps Pink) or Granny Smith, because they hold their shape very well in baking, but by all means use your favorite kind in this recipe.

. . . .

Serves 10 to 12

Chamomile-Infused Milk
Scant cup (225 ml) whole milk

2½ tbsp (15 g) loose-leaf chamomile tea

Chamomile Apple Cake
Cooking spray or butter, for pan

Rounded 1¾ cups (225 g) all-purpose flour

2 tsp (10 g) baking powder

¼ tsp ground cinnamon

¼ tsp fine sea salt

3 tbsp (45 g) sour cream, at room temperature

½ cup + 1½ tbsp (150 g) chamomile-infused milk

½ tsp vanilla extract

½ cup (1 stick; 115 g) unsalted butter, at room temperature

Rounded ¾ cup (175 g) soft light brown sugar

1 tsp finely grated lemon zest

2 large eggs, at room temperature

3 Pink Lady or Granny Smith apples

Whipped cream or vanilla ice cream, for serving (optional)

Make the chamomile-infused milk: In a small saucepan, bring the milk to a simmer. Remove from the heat and add the loose-leaf chamomile tea, give it a stir, cover it with a plate and let it steep for at least 20 to 30 minutes. Strain the milk through a fine-mesh sieve and measure out the ½ cup + 1½ tablespoons (150 g) needed for the cake. Set aside until needed.

Make the cake: Preheat the oven to 350°F (175°C) or 325°F (160°C) if using a fan-assisted oven. Grease a 9-inch (23-cm) round springform pan with cooking spray or butter and line with parchment paper.

Sift the flour, baking powder, cinnamon and salt into a medium-sized bowl and whisk to combine. In a measuring jug, lightly whisk together the sour cream, chamomile-infused milk and vanilla.

In a large bowl, using an electric hand mixer, beat the butter and sugar along with the lemon zest on medium-high speed for 2 to 3 minutes, or until the mixture turns pale and fluffy. Add the eggs, one at a time, making sure each one is fully incorporated before adding the next. Scrape the bowl a couple of times with a silicone spatula to make sure everything is mixed nicely.

Next, add the flour mixture to the butter mixture in three additions, alternating with the sour cream mixture. After each addition, beat the mixture just until everything is incorporated to avoid overmixing the batter. Scrape the batter into the prepared pan and level the top using an offset palette knife.

Peel and core the apples, then cut into quarters. Using a small paring knife, cut the quarters into thin slices, but don't cut all the way through so the quarters stay intact. Arrange the apples, cored side down, tightly on top of the cake batter.

Bake for 50 to 60 minutes. The cake is done when a skewer inserted into the middle comes out mostly clean. When the cake is done, remove it from the oven and let it cool in the pan for about 15 minutes before removing from the pan onto a wire rack to further cool. If desired, serve with some whipped cream or vanilla ice cream while warm.

You can keep the cake in the fridge for several days, covered in plastic wrap or in an airtight container, but take it out of the fridge at least an hour before serving.

Summer on a Plate

Summer: The season with so much beautiful, colorful, delicious produce, yet so little desire to bake or do really anything. I know, the hottest season is not really baking friendly, but the recipes in this chapter are genuinely some of my favorites because I'm a person who loves citrus and fruit desserts.

Although these recipes have all been inspired by summer, you will notice that I use a lot of frozen fruits—that's because I want you to be able to make these recipes any time of the year. Another reason is that I tend to buy fresh produce when it's in season, and then freeze it to have later. While I might prefer using frozen fruits, I've still included tips on how to use fresh produce in these recipes, too.

While the classic Passion Fruit Pavlova (page 113) is always a great, easy choice during the hotter months, you might also want to indulge in the almost-no-bake S'mores Crepe Cake (page 93) with light, chocolate whipped cream filling or the quick and easy Strawberry Cheesecake Swiss Roll (page 100). Or, if you're feeling tropical and you want to create that vacation vibe, choose the amazing Mango Coconut Cake (page 85) or a refreshing but boozy Mojito Cake (page 95) inspired by my favorite cocktail.

Mango **Coconut Cake**

The tropical flavors of this cake are inspired by my trip to Thailand, where I basically lived on mango sticky rice drenched in warm, sweet coconut milk. It was my first time trying mango, and let me tell you—it was love at first taste. Since I wasn't able to buy such perfect mango back home, I chose good-quality mango puree to make the silky mango curd. However, if you have fresh, sweet, ripe mangoes on hand, feel free to make your own puree. I did my best to pack both the cake and the frosting full of delicious coconut flavor, coming through coconut milk, coconut oil and shredded coconut. Triple win!

. . . .

Serves 12 to 14

Mango Curd

9 oz (250 g) mango puree

Juice and zest of 1 lime

Scant ⅔ cup (125 g) granulated sugar

Pinch of salt

3 large egg yolks

1 large egg

¼ cup (½ stick; 60 g) unsalted butter, cold and cubed

Coconut Buttercream

¼ cup + 2 tbsp (45 g) all-purpose flour

1 cup (200 g) granulated sugar

¼ tsp fine sea salt

12 oz (350 g) coconut milk (see Note)

1⅓ cups (2⅔ sticks; 300 g) unsalted butter, at room temperature

½ tsp vanilla extract

Zest of 1 lime

Make the mango curd: In a small saucepan, whisk together the mango puree, lime juice and zest, sugar, salt, egg yolks and egg. Cook over medium-low heat, whisking constantly until the mixture thickens, 5 to 10 minutes. The curd is ready when it can coat the back of a wooden spoon. Once it's done, add the butter and whisk until everything is incorporated and smooth. Strain the curd through a sieve to get rid of any lumps and transfer to a glass jar. Refrigerate for a couple of hours, until it comes to a spreadable consistency.

Begin the buttercream: In a small, heavy-bottomed saucepan, whisk together the flour, sugar, salt and coconut milk. Cook over medium to high heat, whisking constantly so the mixture doesn't burn or catch on the bottom of the pan. Once it starts to thicken and you notice bubbling, cook for another 2 minutes, still whisking constantly, until it resembles pastry cream. This whole process could take up to 10 minutes.

When the pudding base is done, strain it through a sieve onto a shallow plate to get rid of any lumps. Cover it with plastic wrap touching the surface to prevent a skin from forming and let it cool to room temperature. You can speed up the process by letting it cool in the fridge, but prior to using, it must be room temperature.

(continued)

Coconut Cake

Cooking spray or butter, for pans

1¾ cups (220 g) all-purpose flour

2 tsp (10 g) baking powder

½ tsp fine sea salt

Rounded ⅔ cup (60 g) desiccated coconut

5.5 oz (160 g) coconut milk, at room temperature

¼ cup (60 g) sour cream, at room temperature

½ tsp vanilla extract

6 tbsp (¾ stick; 90 g) unsalted butter, at room temperature

¼ cup (60 g) coconut oil, melted and cooled

1¼ cups (250 g) granulated sugar

3 large eggs, at room temperature

Make the cake: Preheat the oven to 350°F (175°C) or 325°F (160°C) if using a fan-assisted oven. Grease three 6-inch (15-cm) round cake pans with cooking spray or butter and line the bottoms with parchment paper.

Sift the flour, baking powder and salt into a medium-sized bowl. Add the desiccated coconut and whisk to combine. In a measuring jug, lightly whisk together the coconut milk, sour cream and vanilla.

Using a stand mixer fitted with the paddle attachment, beat the butter and coconut oil with half of the sugar until pale and fluffy, 2 to 3 minutes. Add the rest of the sugar and beat to combine. Add the eggs, one at a time, making sure each is fully incorporated before adding the next.

Next, add the flour mixture in three additions, alternating with the sour cream mixture to avoid splashing and overmixing the batter. After each addition, mix the batter just until combined. Scrape the bowl a couple of times with a silicone spatula to make sure everything is mixed nicely.

Divide the batter equally by weight among the prepared pans and level it with an offset palette knife, then bake for 22 to 25 minutes. It's best to check the cakes after 22 minutes and then adjust the baking time accordingly, because ovens can vary. The cakes are done when they're springy on the top and when a skewer inserted into the middle comes out mostly clean. Remove the cakes from the oven and leave them to cool in their pans on a wire rack for 10 to 15 minutes to firm up a little bit before removing them from the pans to cool completely.

While the cakes are cooling, finish the buttercream: Using the stand mixer fitted with the paddle attachment, beat the butter for 5 minutes, or until it's pale and fluffy, then add the previously made pudding base, one spoonful at a time. Beat everything until nicely incorporated with no lumps. Lastly, add the vanilla and lime zest and beat for a couple of seconds, or until smooth and combined.

Coconut flakes, for decorating

Assemble the cake: Start by leveling the tops of your cakes using a cake leveler or a long, serrated knife for a neater look, if needed. Then, put a little bit of buttercream in the middle of a serving plate or your cake board to keep the cake from moving around. Place it on a turntable for easier handling and decorating.

Place one cake layer on the serving plate and, using a small, offset palette knife or a piping bag filled with buttercream, spread the frosting over the top of the cake layer, about ¼ inch (6 mm) thick. Make a dam around it and fill with some mango curd. Top it with the next cake layer and repeat the process. Place the final cake layer on top, making sure it's upside down to get a nice, smooth surface on top.

Next, apply a thin layer of frosting around the cake and smooth it using a cake scraper to keep in the crumbs. Chill the cake in the fridge for 30 to 60 minutes before applying the final coat of frosting and decorating.

Once the crumb coat is firm, frost the cake with the remaining buttercream in a rustic manner and decorate the top with toasted coconut flakes, if desired.

Keep the cake tightly covered in plastic wrap or in an airtight container at room temperature for 2 days or in the fridge for up to a week. Allow it to come to room temperature before serving.

Note: Use coconut milk that has at least 70 percent coconut, with water as the only additional ingredient. The best kind comes in a carton, but you can use canned, too.

Cinnamon Spice *Blueberry* Cake

My newfound appreciation for blueberry pie has influenced me in creating this extremely delicious cake. The star of the show has to be the sweet, gooey blueberry filling that I could just eat on its own—it's that good! But luckily, the soft and moist cinnamon spiced cake serves as a worthy vessel, too. With its simple yet romantic design, this cake might just be the summery showstopper you've been looking for.

· ·

Serves 12 to 14

¾ cup (1½ sticks; 170 g) unsalted butter, sliced

Blueberry Pie Filling
12.5 oz (350 g) frozen blueberries (see Note)

Rounded ¼ cup (60 g) granulated sugar

¼ tsp ground cardamom

1 tbsp (15 ml) lemon juice, freshly squeezed

Rounded tbsp (10 g) cornstarch + 1 to 2 tbsp (15 to 30 ml) water

Brown the butter: In a light-colored skillet, melt the sliced butter over medium-high heat, stirring constantly, until it becomes foamy, then turns clear and starts showing brown specks. You'll also notice a nutty aroma. It's done after about 5 minutes, at a medium brown stage. Transfer the butter to a metal bowl and leave at room temperature to firm up. You can also put it in the fridge, but make sure to stir it occasionally so it firms up evenly and gets to a room-temperature consistency.

Make the blueberry pie filling: In a small, heavy-bottomed saucepan, combine the frozen blueberries, granulated sugar, cardamom and lemon juice and bring to a boil over medium heat. Simmer for a few minutes.

In a small bowl, dilute the cornstarch with the water and pour the mixture over the blueberries, stirring constantly with a large wooden spoon until everything is incorporated. Bring the mixture back to a boil and cook for a few minutes, until thick. If the filling is too thick, you can always add some more water—a couple of tablespoons (about 30 ml) at a time. But keep in mind the filling will thicken some more in the fridge.

Once thickened, transfer it to a bowl and cover with plastic wrap touching the surface to prevent a skin from forming. You can put it in the fridge to cool completely.

(continued)

Cinnamon Spice *Blueberry* Cake (Continued)

Blueberry Frosting

⅓ cup (45 g) all-purpose flour

1 cup (200 g) granulated sugar

¼ tsp fine sea salt

1½ cups (360 ml) whole milk

4 to 6 tbsp (60 to 90 ml) blueberry filling

1⅓ cups (2⅔ sticks; 300 g) unsalted butter, at room temperature

½ tsp vanilla extract

Cinnamon Cake

Cooking spray or butter, for pans

2 cups (250 g) all-purpose flour

2 tsp (10 g) baking powder

2 tsp (10 g) ground cinnamon

½ tsp fine sea salt

Rounded ¾ cup (180 g) sour cream, at room temperature

¼ cup (60 ml) whole milk, at room temperature

3 tbsp (45 ml) sunflower oil

½ tsp vanilla extract

Reserved brown butter, at room temperature

Rounded cup (250 g) soft light brown sugar

3 large eggs, at room temperature

Begin the frosting: In a small, heavy-bottomed saucepan, whisk together the flour, granulated sugar, salt and milk. Cook over medium to high heat, whisking constantly so the mixture doesn't burn or catch on the bottom of the pan. Once it starts to thicken and you notice bubbling, cook for another 2 minutes, still whisking constantly, until it resembles pastry cream. This whole process could take up to 10 minutes.

When the pudding base is done, strain it through a sieve onto a shallow plate to get rid of any lumps. Cover it with plastic wrap touching the surface to prevent a skin from forming and let it cool to room temperature. You can speed up the process by letting it cool in the fridge, but prior to using, it must be room temperature.

Make the cake: Preheat the oven to 350°F (175°C) or 325°F (160°C) if using a fan-assisted oven. Grease three 6-inch (15-cm) round cake pans with cooking spray or butter and line the bottoms with parchment paper.

Sift the flour, baking powder, cinnamon and salt into a medium-sized bowl and whisk to combine. In a measuring jug, lightly whisk together the sour cream, milk, sunflower oil and vanilla.

Using a stand mixer fitted with the paddle attachment, beat the reserved brown butter with half of the sugar until fluffy, 2 to 3 minutes. Add the rest of the sugar and beat to combine. Add the eggs, one at a time, making sure each is fully incorporated before adding the next.

Next, add the flour mixture in three additions, alternating with the sour cream mixture to avoid splashing and overmixing the batter. After each addition, mix the batter just until combined. Scrape the bowl a couple of times with a silicone spatula to make sure everything is mixed nicely.

Divide the batter equally by weight among the prepared pans and level it with an offset palette knife, then bake for 22 to 25 minutes. It's best to check the cakes after 22 minutes and then adjust the baking time accordingly, because ovens can vary. The cakes are done when they're springy on the top and when a skewer inserted into the middle comes out mostly clean. When they're done, remove from the oven and leave them to cool in their pans on a wire rack for 10 to 15 minutes to firm up a little bit before removing them from the pans to cool completely.

Fresh blueberries and edible flowers, for decorating (optional)

Finish the frosting: Place the blueberry filling in a small bowl and puree it using an immersion blender. Reserve the rest of the filling for filling the cake. Using the stand mixer fitted with the paddle attachment, beat the butter for 5 minutes, or until it's pale and fluffy, then add the previously made pudding base, one spoonful at a time. Beat everything until nicely incorporated with no lumps. Lastly, add the pureed blueberry filling and vanilla and beat until smooth and combined.

Assemble the cake: Start by leveling the tops of your cakes using a cake leveler or a long, serrated knife for a neater look, if needed. Then, put a little bit of buttercream in the middle of a serving plate or your cake board to keep the cake from moving around. Place it on a turntable for easier handling and decorating.

Place one cake layer on the serving plate and, using a small, offset palette knife or a piping bag filled with buttercream, spread the frosting over the top of the cake layer, about ⅜ inch (1 cm) thick. Make a dam around the edges and fill with a couple of tablespoons of the blueberry pie filling. Top it with the next cake layer and repeat the process. Place the final cake layer on top, making sure it's upside down to get a nice, smooth surface on top.

Next, apply a thin layer of frosting around the cake and smooth it using a cake scraper to keep in the crumbs. Chill the cake in the fridge for 30 to 60 minutes before applying the final coat of frosting and decorating.

Once the crumb coat is firm, frost the cake with the remaining buttercream and smooth the sides and the top using a cake scraper. Create a swirly effect by gently pressing the back of the palette knife from bottom to top and creating slight diagonal lines. Decorate the top in the same manner. Decorate the top with fresh blueberries and edible flowers, if desired.

Keep the cake tightly covered in plastic wrap or in an airtight container at room temperature for 2 days or in the fridge for up to a week. Allow it to come to room temperature before serving.

Note: You'll notice that in most of my recipes I use frozen fruit, and that's because they are almost always available. However, you can most certainly use the fresh ones when in season; just make sure to add a few tablespoons (30 to 60 ml) of water to replace the liquid that melts from the frozen fruit, which helps dissolve the sugar.

 Crepe Cake

Crepes are probably the first sweet thing I learned to make. We call them *palačinke,* and I've made thousands of them so far, but never using a recipe, just a feeling for texture. So, I actually loved that making this s'mores-inspired crepe cake challenged me to measure everything and finally write it down. To bring the s'mores element, I filled the cake with a light, whipped cream–based chocolate filling, crushed graham crackers for a little crunch and then the mound of sweet, torched meringue on top. Sounds like a perfect, chocoholic's summer dessert to me, and I hope you'll agree.

Serves 8 to 10

Crepes

3 large eggs, at room temperature

3 tbsp (45 g) granulated sugar

¼ tsp fine sea salt

2 cups (250 g) all-purpose flour

1¾ cups (420 ml) whole milk, at room temperature

1 cup (240 ml) sparkling water

1 tbsp (15 ml) dark rum (optional, see Notes)

Finely grated zest of ½ lemon

Sunflower oil, for pan

Filling

5.5 oz (150 g) 55% dark chocolate

¼ cup (30 g) Dutch-processed cocoa powder

5 tbsp (75 ml) hot water

11.5 oz (320 g) mascarpone cheese, cold

Rounded ¾ cup (100 g) powdered sugar

1 tsp vanilla extract

1½ cups (360 ml) heavy cream, cold

Make the crepes: In a large bowl, vigorously whisk together the eggs, granulated sugar and salt for 30 to 60 seconds. Add the flour, milk and sparkling water in batches, alternating among the three ingredients and whisking constantly so the mixture is always smooth with no lumps. Add the rum (if using) and the lemon zest, whisk to combine and place the batter in the fridge, covered tightly, for at least 30 minutes or up to 1 day.

Place a 9-inch (23-cm) crepe pan over medium-high heat and fill liberally with the sunflower oil. Once the pan gets hot and the oil is thin, pour the excess oil into a small heatproof bowl or coffee cup. Pour a ladleful of the batter into the middle of the hot pan and twirl or tilt the pan in the air quickly, off the heat, to distribute the batter evenly across the whole pan. Place the pan back over medium-high heat and cook for about 1 minute, or until the bottom is set and the top isn't shiny and liquid anymore. Flip onto the other side and cook for another 15 to 30 seconds. Transfer the cooked crepe to a large plate. Repeat with the rest of the batter, but make sure to oil the pan before each new crepe by sprinkling the pan with a few drops of the reserved oil and tilting to spread it all over the pan. Stack the successive crepes on the same plate when cooked. This recipe will make about 20 crepes if you are using a 9-inch (23-cm) pan.

When you've used up all the batter, leave the crepes to cool to room temperature, covered loosely to avoid condensation.

Make the filling: Melt the chocolate in a heatproof bowl set over a pan of simmering water, then set aside to slightly cool. In a small bowl, combine the cocoa powder with the water, whisk until smooth and combined and set aside until needed. In a large bowl, using an electric hand mixer, beat the mascarpone cheese with the powdered sugar and vanilla until combined. Add the cocoa powder mixture and melted chocolate, and beat until fully incorporated. In a separate large bowl, beat the cream to medium soft peak stage, then gradually fold it into the cheese mixture using a silicone spatula.

(continued)

Meringue Topping
2.8 oz (80 g) egg whites (about 2 eggs)

1 cup (200 g) granulated sugar

½ tsp fine sea salt

½ tsp vanilla extract

2 oz (60 g) graham crackers or digestive cookies, ground

Chocolate Ganache
3.5 oz (100 g) 55% dark chocolate, finely chopped

½ cup (125 g) heavy cream

Notes: My grandma taught me that if you put a little bit of alcohol in the batter, your crepes shouldn't come out greasy. I don't know if that's entirely true, but I adore rum, so it's a nonnegotiable ingredient in my crepes. However, feel free to leave it out if you don't like it.

I always make crepes with a whisk, because that's how I've been doing it forever, but feel free to use an electric hand mixer. You can also use a bigger or a smaller skillet; you'll just end up with more or fewer crepes.

It's an unwritten rule that the first crepe is always bad, so don't worry. Use the first couple of tries to figure out how much batter you need in your ladle to cover the pan completely while keeping the crepes as thin as possible.

Make the meringue topping: In the bowl of a stand mixer, whisk together the egg whites, granulated sugar and salt. Place the bowl over a pot of simmering water, but make sure the bowl doesn't touch the water. Heat the egg white mixture, whisking constantly, until the sugar completely dissolves, 2 to 4 minutes. Ideally, the mixture should reach 160°F (70°C), but if you don't have a thermometer, just make sure the mixture is smooth and hot. You can check whether the sugar is dissolved by rubbing some of the mixture between your fingers.

Carefully wipe the bottom of the hot bowl and place it on the stand mixer fitted with the whisk attachment. Beat the meringue on high speed until it reaches stiff peaks and is no longer hot to the touch. Depending on your mixer, this could take up to 10 to 15 minutes. After you've reached the glossy, stiff peak stage, turn off the mixer, add the vanilla and beat for another 15 seconds, or just until incorporated. Set aside.

Assemble the cake: Dab a little bit of the filling onto a cake stand or a serving plate so the crepes won't move. Place one crepe on the stand and spread a thin layer of filling all over, about 3 tablespoons (45 ml), and then sprinkle with about a tablespoon (15 g) of ground graham crackers. Repeat this process until you've used all the crepes. Chill for 30 to 60 minutes before adding the meringue topping and ganache.

Make the chocolate ganache: Place the chocolate in a small, heatproof bowl. In a small saucepan, bring the cream to a simmer, then pour it over the chocolate. Cover with a plate and let sit for 1 to 2 minutes, or until the chocolate softens and begins to melt. Stir with a spatula until combined and smooth. Alternatively, you can do this (using a microwave-safe bowl) in a microwave in 30-second intervals. Pour the ganache on the middle of the stacked crepes and spread to the edges using an offset palette knife. Place in the fridge for 30 minutes, or until the ganache sets a little bit. Then, spoon the meringue on top in a rustic manner and torch with a blowtorch.

Keep the cake tightly covered in the fridge for 2 to 3 days.

 Cake

Along with coffee desserts, I have a big spot in my heart for boozy ones as well. I was very excited about this cake, because a good mojito is actually my favorite summer cocktail. I didn't want to use extracts, because that just wouldn't cut it for me. Instead, the mint tea–infused milk absolutely did the trick. Mixed with lime juice and zest, this cake turned out to be the perfect combination of sweet and fresh flavor with soft and moist texture. With the silky, brown sugar rum frosting on top, everything comes together to taste just like a mojito.

Serves 12 to 14

Mint Tea–Infused Milk
1 cup (240 ml) whole milk
5 tsp (10 g) loose-leaf mint tea

Brown Sugar Rum Buttercream
¼ cup + 2 tbsp (45 g) all-purpose flour
¾ cup + 2 tbsp (200 g) soft light brown sugar
¼ tsp fine sea salt
1½ cups (360 ml) whole milk
1⅓ cups (2⅔ sticks; 300 g) unsalted butter, at room temperature
Scant to rounded ¼ cup (60 to 80 g) dark rum (see Note)

Mojito Cake
Cooking spray or butter, for pans
2 cups (250 g) all-purpose flour
2 tsp (10 g) baking powder
½ tsp fine sea salt
½ cup (120 ml) mint tea–infused milk
⅓ cup (80 g) sour cream, at room temperature
3 tbsp (45 ml) sunflower oil
2 tbsp (30 ml) fresh lime juice
Zest of 2 limes
½ cup (1 stick; 115 g) unsalted butter, at room temperature
1 cup (200 g) granulated sugar
Scant ¼ cup (50 g) soft light brown sugar
3 large eggs, at room temperature

Make the mint tea–infused milk: In a small saucepan, bring the milk to a simmer over medium-high heat. Remove from the heat, add the loose-leaf mint tea and give it a stir. Cover with a plate and let steep for at least 20 minutes, or until it comes to room temperature. Strain it through a sieve and set aside.

Begin the buttercream: In a small, heavy-bottomed saucepan, whisk together the flour, brown sugar, salt and milk. Cook over medium to high heat, whisking constantly so it doesn't burn or catch on the bottom of the pan. Once it starts to thicken and you notice bubbling, cook for another 2 minutes, still whisking constantly, until it resembles pastry cream. This whole process could take up to 10 minutes.

When the pudding base is done, strain it through a sieve onto a shallow plate to get rid of any lumps. Cover it with plastic wrap touching the surface to prevent a skin from forming and let it cool to room temperature. You can speed up the process by letting it cool in the fridge, but prior to using, it must be room temperature.

Make the cake: Preheat the oven to 350°F (175°C) or 325°F (160°C) if using a fan-assisted oven. Grease three 6-inch (15-cm) round cake pans with cooking spray or butter and line the bottoms with parchment paper.

Sift the flour, baking powder and salt into a medium-sized bowl and whisk to combine. In a measuring jug, lightly whisk together the mint-infused milk, sour cream, sunflower oil, lime juice and zest.

Using a stand mixer fitted with the paddle attachment, beat the butter with half of the granulated sugar until pale and fluffy, 2 to 3 minutes. Add the rest of the sugar and the brown sugar and beat to combine. Add the eggs, one at a time, making sure each is fully incorporated before adding the next.

Next, add the flour mixture in three additions, alternating with the sour cream mixture to avoid splashing and overmixing the batter. After each addition, mix the batter just until combined. Scrape the bowl a couple of times with a silicone spatula to make sure everything is mixed nicely.

(continued)

Lime slices, fresh mint leaves and demerara sugar, for decorating (optional)

Note: If you don't want to use rum, that's okay. You can either omit it completely or use some lime zest and juice instead.

Divide the batter equally by weight among the prepared pans and level with an offset palette knife, then bake for 22 to 25 minutes. It's best to check the cakes after 22 minutes and then adjust the baking time accordingly, because ovens can vary. The cakes are done when they're springy on the top and when a skewer inserted into the middle comes out mostly clean. Remove them from the oven and leave them to cool in their pans on a wire rack for 10 to 15 minutes to firm up a little bit before removing them from the pans to cool completely.

While the cakes are cooling, finish the buttercream: Using the stand mixer fitted with the paddle attachment, beat the butter for 5 minutes, or until it's pale and fluffy, then add the previously made pudding base, one spoonful at a time. Beat everything until nicely incorporated with no lumps. Lastly, add the rum and beat for a couple of seconds, until smooth and combined.

Assemble the cake: Start by leveling the tops of your cakes using a cake leveler or a long, serrated knife for a neater look, if needed. Then, put a little bit of buttercream in the middle of a serving plate or your cake board to keep the cake from moving around. Place it on a turntable for easier handling and decorating.

Place one cake layer on the serving plate and, using a small, offset palette knife or a piping bag filled with buttercream, spread the frosting over the top of the cake layer, about ⅜ inch (1 cm) thick. Top it with the next cake layer and repeat the process. Place the final cake layer on top, making sure it's upside down to get a nice, smooth surface on top.

Next, apply a thin layer of frosting around the cake and smooth it using a cake scraper to keep in the crumbs. Chill the cake in the fridge for 30 to 60 minutes before applying the final coat of frosting and decorating.

Once the crumb coat is firm, place the cake on the turntable, frost with the remaining buttercream and smooth the sides and the top using a cake scraper. To create the swirl effect, place the tip of an offset palette knife on the bottom of the cake, holding it parallel to the sides of the cake. Keep a gentle pressure and pull the palette knife to the top while spinning the turntable.

Decorate with lime slices, fresh mint leaves and demerara sugar on top, if desired.

Keep the cake tightly covered in plastic wrap or in an airtight container at room temperature for 2 days or in the fridge for up to a week. Allow it to come to room temperature before serving.

Raspberry Almond Crumble Cake

Even though I love making layer cakes, sometimes all you need is a simple, quick, delicious dessert, and that's exactly what this Raspberry Almond Crumble Cake is all about. It's tender, moist, buttery and topped with my favorite fruit and crunchy streusel. It can almost pass for a breakfast meal, right? For a richer flavor, don't skip toasting the nuts. Trust me, it makes all the difference.

. . . .

Serves 10 to 12

Streusel

Scant ¾ cup (90 g) all-purpose flour

¼ tsp fine sea salt

¼ cup (60 g) soft light brown sugar

¼ cup (½ stick; 55 g) unsalted butter, melted

Cake

Cooking spray or butter, for pan

Scant 1¼ cups (150 g) all-purpose flour

1¾ tsp (8.5 g) baking powder

¼ tsp ground cinnamon

½ tsp fine sea salt

Rounded ¾ cup (75 g) ground almonds, toasted

Rounded ½ cup (120 g) sour cream, at room temperature

3 tbsp (45 ml) sunflower oil

¼ cup (60 ml) whole milk, at room temperature

½ tsp vanilla extract

6 tbsp (¾ stick; 90 g) unsalted butter, at room temperature

⅔ cup (150 g) soft light brown sugar

2 large eggs, at room temperature

5.5 oz (150 g) fresh or frozen raspberries (see Note)

Powdered sugar, for dusting

Make the streusel: Sift the flour, salt and brown sugar in a medium-sized bowl and whisk to combine. Gradually add the melted butter while stirring with a fork, until the mixture starts clumping together. Put in the fridge until needed.

Make the cake: Preheat the oven to 350°F (175°C) or 325°F (160°C) if using a fan-assisted oven. Grease with cooking spray or butter and line a 9-inch (23-cm) round springform pan with parchment paper.

Sift the flour, baking powder, cinnamon and salt into a medium-sized bowl. Add the toasted ground almonds and whisk to combine. In a measuring jug, lightly whisk together the sour cream, sunflower oil, milk and vanilla.

In a large bowl, using an electric hand mixer, beat the butter and brown sugar on medium-high speed for 2 to 3 minutes, or until it turns pale and fluffy. Add the eggs, one at a time, making sure each is fully combined before adding the next. Scrape the bowl a couple of times with a silicone spatula to make sure everything is getting mixed nicely.

Next, add the flour mixture in three additions, alternating with the sour cream mixture. After each addition, beat the mixture just until everything is incorporated to avoid overmixing the batter. Scrape the batter into the prepared pan and spread evenly. Scatter the raspberries on top and sprinkle with the streusel.

Bake for 40 to 45 minutes. The cake is done when it's springy on the top and when a skewer inserted into the middle comes out mostly clean. Once the cake is done, remove from the oven and let it cool in the pan placed on a wire rack for about 15 minutes before removing from the pan to firm up and cool further, or to room temperature. Once cooled, place it onto a serving plate and dust with a little bit of powdered sugar.

The cake is best when served the same day and still just slightly warm. You can keep the cake in the fridge for several days, covered in plastic wrap or in an airtight container, but take it out of the fridge at least an hour before serving.

Note: The cake works with both fresh and frozen raspberries. If using frozen ones, don't defrost them.

Strawberry **Cheesecake Swiss Roll**

In this exquisite rolled cake, we have a classic flavor in its fanciest form. My family jumps at the mention of strawberries or cheesecake, so this pairing had to happen. It's a really great choice for summer desserts, because the sponge is very light and airy, perfect for hot summer days. I chose to sweeten the cream cheese filling with white chocolate, which makes it both creamy and tangy, and most important, not overly sweet. For the strawberry part, I decided to make a quick jam, which is my favorite way of incorporating fruit into desserts. But feel free to sprinkle finely chopped fresh strawberries over the filling. The best part is that you can make this cake with fresh or frozen berries, which means you can enjoy this strawberry cheesecake roll throughout the year.

. . . .

Serves 10 to 12

Cake
Cooking spray or butter, for baking sheet

Rounded ¾ cup (100 g) all-purpose flour

¾ tsp baking powder

¼ tsp fine sea salt

4 large eggs, at room temperature

¾ cup (150 g) granulated sugar

Zest of 1 lemon

1 tsp vanilla extract

2 tbsp (30 ml) sunflower oil

Powdered sugar, for dusting

Strawberry Jam
10.5 oz (300 g) fresh or frozen strawberries, plus more for decorating

3 tbsp (40 g) granulated sugar

1 tbsp (15 ml) water

Make the cake: Preheat the oven to 350°F (175°C) or 325°F (160°C) if using a fan-assisted oven. Grease with cooking spray or butter and line with parchment paper a 10 x 15–inch (25 x 38–cm) baking sheet. Lightly grease the parchment paper, too.

Sift the flour, baking powder and salt into a medium-sized bowl, whisk together and set aside. In a bowl of a stand mixer fitted with the whisk attachment, beat together the eggs, granulated sugar, lemon zest and vanilla on medium-high speed for a couple of minutes, or until the mixture becomes pale and doubles in size. Then, add the sunflower oil and mix until well incorporated. Lastly, gradually fold in the flour mixture until everything is combined.

Pour the batter into the prepared baking sheet and spread evenly all the way into the corners using an offset palette knife. Bake for 12 to 15 minutes, or until a toothpick inserted into the middle comes out clean. Check after 12 minutes and then adjust the baking time accordingly.

Generously sprinkle a clean kitchen towel or a large piece of nonstick parchment paper with powdered sugar. This prevents the cake from sticking to the towel. When the cake is done baking, remove the pan from the oven, leave it for 1 minute in the pan and flip the cake onto the towel. Carefully remove the parchment paper and dust the cake with powdered sugar. While still hot, roll up the cake in the towel. It's imperative to do it while still hot, otherwise it will crack later.

Make the strawberry jam: In a small saucepan, bring the strawberries, granulated sugar and water to a simmer on medium-high heat, stirring occasionally so the mixture doesn't catch on the bottom of the pan. Press the strawberries with the back of the silicone spatula or a wooden spoon to speed up the process. Simmer until the mixture is thick, 15 to 20 minutes. Remove from the heat, strain it through a sieve or puree it with an immersion blender, cover with plastic wrap touching the surface to prevent a skin from forming and let cool completely before using.

(continued)

Strawberry Cheesecake Filling

3.5 oz (100 g) white chocolate, finely chopped

7 oz (200 g) cream cheese

4.5 oz (125 g) mascarpone cheese

3 to 4 tbsp (45 to 60 ml) strawberry jam

½ cup + 1½ tbsp (150 g) heavy cream

Raspberries, for decorating

Make the strawberry cheesecake filling: Melt the white chocolate in a heatproof bowl set over a pot of simmering water and let it cool to room temperature.

Using a large bowl and a hand mixer or a stand mixer with a whisk attachment, mix together the cream cheese and mascarpone cheese with the strawberry jam until smooth and combined, reserving the remaining jam for assembling the cake. Add the cooled melted white chocolate and mix until everything is creamy and incorporated. In a separate bowl, beat the cream until soft peaks form. Carefully fold the whipped cream into the cheese mixture, until evenly combined.

The filling will be a little soft. If it feels too soft, chill it for 10 to 15 minutes in the fridge before spreading it over the cake.

Assemble the cake: Unroll the cooled cake carefully and spread evenly with a thin layer of the reserved strawberry jam. Then, spread the strawberry cream cheese filling on top of the jam using an offset palette knife. Carefully roll the cake back up. Refrigerate for at least 2 hours before serving.

Sprinkle with more powdered sugar before serving, cut the ends for a neater look and decorate with fresh raspberries, strawberries or other berries, if desired. Keep the cake in the fridge, tightly covered with plastic wrap to avoid drying the cake.

Roasted *Plum* Tonka Cupcakes

I feel that plums are the underdog of summer fruit and I don't know why. My mum has loads of plums in her orchard, so we always had some plum jam on hand when I was growing up. I've only recently discovered the magic of roasting fruit, thanks to my friend Mateja, and it's a real game changer for bringing out the extra caramelly notes that make this puree exceptional. If you've never heard of tonka bean before, it looks like a little black, wrinkled bean. Its taste or, more accurately, scent is sweet, but also earthy, creamy and spicy. Kind of like a mix of different aromas: vanilla, cinnamon, nutmeg, cherry . . . but with a tonka twist. It goes really wonderful with stone fruit, such as plums.

. . . .

Serves 12

Roasted Plum Puree
21 oz (600 g) plums, stoned and halved, plus more for topping

3 tbsp (45 g) soft light brown sugar

2 tbsp (30 ml) fresh lemon juice

Plum Buttercream
3 tbsp + 1 tsp (25 g) all-purpose flour

Scant ⅔ cup (120 g) granulated sugar

Pinch of salt

¾ cup + 1 tbsp (195 ml) whole milk

¾ cup + 1 tbsp (1½ sticks + 1 tbsp; 185 g) unsalted butter, at room temperature

3 to 4 tbsp (45 to 60 ml) plum puree

Roast the plums: Preheat the oven to 375°F (190°C) or 350°F (175°C) if using a fan-assisted oven. Place the plums, cut side up, on a rimmed baking sheet and sprinkle with the sugar and lemon juice. Bake for 20 to 30 minutes, or until the plums become soft, slightly caramelized and release their juices. Once the plums are ready, transfer them, along with all the juices, to a heatproof measuring jug and blend using an immersion blender, until smooth. Transfer the puree to a glass jar and set aside until needed.

Begin the buttercream: In a small, heavy-bottomed saucepan, whisk together the flour, sugar, salt and milk. Cook over medium to high heat, whisking constantly so the mixture doesn't burn or catch on the bottom of the pan. Once it starts to thicken and you notice bubbling, cook for another 2 minutes, still whisking constantly, until it resembles pastry cream. This whole process could take up to 10 minutes.

When the pudding base is done, strain it through a sieve onto a shallow plate to get rid of any lumps. Cover it with plastic wrap touching the surface to prevent a skin from forming and let it cool to room temperature. You can speed up the process by letting it cool in the fridge, but prior to using, it must be room temperature.

(continued)

. . . .

Tonka Cupcakes

1⅔ cups (200 g) all-purpose flour

Rounded cup (225 g) granulated sugar

1¾ tsp (9 g) baking powder

¼ tsp fine sea salt

1 small tonka bean (see Note)

Rounded ¾ cup (180 g) sour cream, at room temperature

3 tbsp (45 ml) sunflower oil

2 large eggs, at room temperature

½ tsp vanilla extract

6 tbsp (¾ stick; 85 g) unsalted butter, at room temperature

Make the cupcakes: Preheat the oven to 350°F (175°C) or 325°F (160°C) if using a fan-assisted oven. Line a cupcake pan with 12 paper liners.

Sift the flour, sugar, baking powder and salt into the bowl of a stand mixer, or a medium-sized bowl if using an electric hand mixer. Grate the tonka bean directly into the bowl and whisk to combine. In a measuring jug, lightly whisk together the sour cream, sunflower oil, eggs and vanilla. Add the butter to the flour mixture, fit the stand mixer with the paddle attachment and mix on low speed until you get a sandlike texture and there are no traces of flour.

Next, add the sour cream mixture in two equal batches to avoid splashing and overmixing the cake. After each addition, mix the batter on low speed for about 15 seconds, or until everything is fully incorporated. Scrape the bowl a couple of times with a silicone spatula to make sure everything is mixed nicely.

Fill the prepared paper liners three-quarters of the way full and bake for 18 to 20 minutes. The cupcakes are done if they spring back when lightly touched or when a toothpick inserted into the middle of a cupcake comes out mostly clean. Remove from the oven and let the cupcakes firm up in the pan for 2 to 3 minutes before transferring them to a wire rack to cool completely.

While the cupcakes are cooling, finish the buttercream: Using a stand mixer fitted with the paddle attachment, beat the butter for 5 minutes, or until it's pale and fluffy, then add the previously made pudding base, one spoonful at a time. Beat everything until nicely incorporated with no lumps. Lastly, add the plum puree and beat for a couple of seconds, until smooth and combined.

Assemble the cupcakes: Make a hole in the center of each cupcake using an apple corer and fill with plum puree. Transfer the buttercream to a piping bag fitted with a small petal nozzle and pipe little petals all around to create a flower. Top with fresh, sliced plums, if desired.

The cupcakes are best when served the same day at room temperature, but you can keep them in the fridge in an airtight container for 2 to 3 days.

Note: You can find tonka beans in specialty spice stores or online.

Lemon Meringue **Pie Cake**

As an avid lemon lover, this cake has to be in my top five cakes of all time. Here, you'll find lemon at every stage of the cake: It's in the cake layers, in the filling and in the frosting. It's packed full with zesty lemon flavor, and I wouldn't want it any other way. To bring a touch of pie style to this recipe, the cake is also filled with delicious, golden nuggets of buttery pie dough and topped with sweet, torched meringue.

. . . .

Serves 12 to 14

Lemon Curd

4 large egg yolks

1 large egg

Rounded ¾ cup (160 g) granulated sugar

½ cup (125 g) fresh lemon juice

Finely grated zest of 2 lemons

¼ cup (½ stick; 55 g) unsalted butter, cold and cubed

Lemon Buttercream

¼ cup + 2 tbsp (45 g) all-purpose flour

1 cup (200 g) granulated sugar

¼ tsp fine sea salt

1½ cups (360 ml) whole milk

1⅓ cups (2⅔ sticks; 300 g) unsalted butter, at room temperature

Finely grated zest of 2 lemons

3 to 4 tbsp (45 to 60 ml) lemon curd

Lemon Cake

Cooking spray or butter, for pans

2 cups (250 g) all-purpose flour

2 tsp (10 g) baking powder

½ tsp fine sea salt

Rounded ¾ cup (180 g) sour cream, at room temperature

3 tbsp (45 ml) sunflower oil

5 tbsp (75 g) fresh lemon juice

½ cup (1 stick; 115 g) unsalted butter, at room temperature

Finely grated zest of 2 lemons

1¼ cups (250 g) granulated sugar

3 large eggs, at room temperature

Make the lemon curd: In a heatproof glass bowl, whisk together the egg yolks, egg, sugar, lemon juice and zest (see Notes). Place over a pan of simmering water, making sure the bowl doesn't touch the water. Cook, whisking constantly, until the mixture thickens, 10 to 15 minutes. The curd is ready when it can coat the back of a wooden spoon. Once it's done, add the butter and whisk until everything is incorporated and smooth. Strain the curd through a sieve to get rid of any possible lumps and transfer to a glass jar. Refrigerate for a couple of hours, or until it comes to a spreadable consistency.

Begin the buttercream: In a small, heavy-bottomed saucepan, whisk together the flour, sugar, salt and milk. Cook over medium to high heat, whisking constantly so the mixture doesn't burn or catch on the bottom of the pan. Once it starts to thicken and you notice bubbling, cook for another 2 minutes, still whisking constantly, until it resembles pastry cream. This whole process could take up to 10 minutes.

When the pudding base is done, strain it through a sieve onto a shallow plate to get rid of any lumps. Cover it with plastic wrap touching the surface to prevent a skin from forming and let it cool to room temperature. You can speed up the process by letting it cool in the fridge, but prior to using, it must be room temperature.

Make the cake: Preheat the oven to 350°F (175°C) or 325°F (160°C) if using a fan-assisted oven. Grease three 6-inch (15-cm) round cake pans with cooking spray or butter and line the bottoms with parchment paper.

Sift the flour, baking powder and salt into a medium-sized bowl and whisk to combine. In a measuring jug, lightly whisk together the sour cream, sunflower oil and lemon juice.

Using a stand mixer fitted with the paddle attachment, beat the butter and lemon zest with half of the sugar until pale and fluffy, 2 to 3 minutes. Add the rest of the sugar and beat to combine. Add the eggs, one at a time, making sure each is fully incorporated before adding the next.

(continued)

Pie Crumb

1 cup (125 g) all-purpose flour

3 tbsp (40 g) granulated sugar

Pinch of salt

⅓ cup (⅔ stick; 75 g) unsalted butter, melted

Next, add the flour mixture in three additions, alternating with the sour cream mixture to avoid splashing and overmixing the batter. After each addition, mix the batter just until combined. Scrape the bowl a couple of times with a silicone spatula to make sure everything is mixed nicely.

Divide the batter equally by weight among the prepared pans and level it with an offset palette knife, then bake for 22 to 25 minutes. It's best to check the cakes after 22 minutes and then adjust the baking time accordingly, because ovens can vary. The cakes are done when they're springy on the top and when a skewer inserted into the middle comes out mostly clean. When they're done, remove them from the oven and leave them to cool in their pans on a wire rack for 10 to 15 minutes to firm up a little bit before removing them from the pans to cool completely.

While the cakes are cooling, prepare the pie crumb: Preheat the oven to 400°F (205°C) or 375°F (190°C) if using a fan-assisted oven.

Sift the flour, sugar and salt into a small mixing bowl and combine together with a fork. Add the melted butter and vigorously "cut" the mixture using a fork until it starts to look like little nuggets of dough.

Spread the dough nuggets on a rimmed baking sheet lined with parchment paper, breaking them into smaller pieces if necessary. Bake for 15 to 20 minutes, or until golden brown on the outside. Remove them from the oven and allow to cool completely before using.

Finish the buttercream: Using the stand mixer fitted with the paddle attachment, beat the butter for 5 minutes, or until it's pale and fluffy, then add the previously made pudding base, one spoonful at a time. Beat everything until nicely incorporated with no lumps. Lastly, add the lemon zest with the lemon curd, reserving the rest of the curd to fill the cake, and beat until smooth and combined.

Assemble the cake: Start by leveling the tops of your cakes using a cake leveler or a long, serrated knife for a neater look, if needed. Then, put a little bit of buttercream in the middle of a serving plate or your cake board to keep the cake from moving around. Place it on a turntable for easier handling and decorating.

Meringue

4 large egg whites

Pinch of salt

1 cup (200 g) superfine sugar

Yellow gel food coloring, for tinting your buttercream

Notes: When making lemon curd, don't use cheap metal equipment, because it will react with the lemon and your lemon curd will end up with a metallic taste. If possible, use a glass bowl and good-quality, stainless-steel whisk.

The pie crumb will get soggy after a couple of days.

Place one cake layer on the serving plate and, using a small, offset palette knife or a piping bag filled with buttercream, spread the frosting over the top of the cake layer, about ¼ inch (6 mm) thick. Make a dam around it and fill with a couple of tablespoons (about 30 ml) of the remaining lemon curd and scatter some of the pie crumb over it. Top it with the next cake layer and repeat the process. Place the final cake layer on top, making sure it's upside down to get a nice, smooth surface on top.

Next, apply a thin layer of frosting around the cake and smooth it using a cake scraper to keep in the crumbs. Chill the cake in the fridge for 30 to 60 minutes before applying the final coat of frosting and decorating. Once the crumb coat is firm, frost the cake with the remaining buttercream, reserving 2 to 3 tablespoons (32 to 48 g) for the next step, and smooth the top and the sides using a cake scraper and an offset palette knife.

Chill the cake for 30 to 60 minutes, or until firm. In the meantime, tint the reserved buttercream two shades of yellow using yellow gel food coloring. Take the cake from the fridge and dab some of the yellow frosting in each shade on the sides of the cake using an offset palette knife. Gently smooth it using a cake scraper for a textured watercolor effect.

Place the cake in the fridge and make the meringue: Before starting the meringue, make sure to wipe your stand mixer bowl and the whisk attachment with some vinegar and paper towels to get rid of any residual grease. Then, using the stand mixer fitted with the whisk attachment, beat the egg whites with a pinch of salt on high speed until soft peaks form. Lower the speed to medium-low and with the mixer still going, add the superfine sugar, one spoonful at a time. Once all the sugar is added, beat on high speed until the sugar is completely dissolved.

To decorate the cake, put the meringue into a large piping bag fitted with a large round nozzle and pipe dollops on top of the cake. When finished, slightly torch the meringue using a blowtorch. Add some pie crumb nuggets around the cake, if desired.

Keep the cake tightly covered in plastic wrap or in an airtight container at room temperature for 2 days or in the fridge for up to a week. Allow it to come to room temperature before serving.

Brown Butter *Nectarine* (Upside-Down) Cake

Nectarines will always remind me of the summers my brother, sister and I spent on a boat with my grandparents. Each afternoon after yet another tiring swimming session, we would eat some kind of fruit, with nectarines and watermelon being our favorite. My grandmother also introduced us to brown butter, which we all adored in her special sauce served with polenta. So, this cake is the combination of some of my dearest childhood memories and is just as delicious as it sounds. Browning the butter gives the cake a nice, nutty aroma, and the nectarines are sprinkled with spiced sugar to make them extra sweet, sticky and caramelized.

Serves 8 to 10

Brown Butter
½ cup + 3 tbsp (1 stick + 3 tbsp; 160 g) unsalted butter, sliced

Fruit Base
3 to 4 nectarines (see Note)
5 tbsp (65 g) granulated sugar
1 tsp ground cardamom
¼ tsp ground cinnamon

Brown Butter Cake
Cooking spray or butter, for pan
1⅔ cups (200 g) all-purpose flour
1½ tsp (7.5 g) baking powder
¼ tsp fine sea salt
Rounded ¾ cup (180 g) sour cream, at room temperature
3 tbsp (45 ml) whole milk, at room temperature
½ tsp vanilla extract
½ cup (120 g) brown butter, at room temperature
¾ cup + 2 tbsp (175 g) granulated sugar
2 large eggs, at room temperature

Brown the butter: In a light-colored skillet, melt the sliced butter over medium-high heat, stirring constantly, until it becomes foamy, then turns clear and starts showing brown specks. You'll also notice a nutty aroma. Your butter is done after about 5 minutes, at a medium brown stage. Transfer the butter to a metal bowl to firm up at room temperature. Alternatively, place it in the fridge to firm up, but make sure to stir it occasionally so it firms up evenly and gets to a room-temperature consistency.

In the meantime, prepare the fruit: Remove the stones from the nectarines and cut them into quarters before slicing into ⅛-inch (3-mm)-thick slices. In a small bowl, combine the sugar, cardamom and cinnamon until the sugar is evenly coated with the spices.

Make the cake: Preheat the oven to 350°F (175°C) or 325°F (160°C) if using a fan-assisted oven. Grease with cooking spray or butter and line with parchment paper a 9-inch (23-cm) round cake pan. Sprinkle 3 tablespoons (40 g) of the spiced sugar on the bottom of the pan and cover with the nectarine slices in a round pattern. Sprinkle the rest of the sugar on top of the nectarines.

Sift the flour, baking powder and salt into a medium-sized bowl and whisk to combine. In a measuring jug, lightly whisk together the sour cream, milk and vanilla.

Using an electric hand mixer, beat together the brown butter and sugar for 2 to 3 minutes on medium-high speed, or until the mixture turns pale and fluffy. Add the eggs, one at a time, making sure each is fully combined before adding the next. Scrape the bowl a couple of times with a silicone spatula to make sure everything is mixed nicely.

(continued)

Brown Butter *Nectarine* (Upside-Down) Cake
(Continued)

Whipped cream, for serving

Next, add the flour mixture to the brown butter mixture in three additions, alternating with the sour cream mixture. After each addition beat the mixture just until everything is incorporated to avoid overmixing the cake. Scrape the batter carefully over the nectarines and level the top using an offset palette knife.

Bake for about 30 minutes. The cake is done when it's springy on the top and when a skewer inserted into the middle comes out mostly clean. Once the cake is done, remove it from the oven and let it cool in the pan on a wire rack for about 15 minutes before turning it upside down onto a serving plate to cool to room temperature. Serve with whipped cream.

The cake is best when served the same day and still just slightly warm. You can keep the cake in the fridge for several days, covered in plastic wrap or in an airtight container, but take it out of the fridge at least an hour before serving.

Note: If you don't have nectarines, you can use peaches or even plums and apricots. Make sure the fruit is ripe enough so you can remove the stone without damaging the fruit and get the most flavor.

 **Pavlova**

Along with Bundt cakes, classic Australian pavlova makes a stunning, impressive dessert with little to no effort. Sweet and mellow meringue is the perfect base for a slightly sour topping, such as the passion fruit curd featured here and, of course, lots and lots of seasonal fruit. Discover your passion for passion fruit with this delicious and beautiful creation!

Serves 8 to 10

Passion Fruit Curd
7 oz (200 g) passion fruit puree

2 tbsp (30 ml) fresh lemon juice

Scant ⅔ cup (125 g) granulated sugar

Pinch of salt

5 large egg yolks

⅓ cup (⅔ stick; 75 g) unsalted butter, cold and cubed

Meringue
5 large egg whites

1¼ cups (250 g) granulated sugar

¼ tsp fine sea salt

1 tsp vanilla extract

1 tsp white vinegar

Rounded tbsp (10 g) cornstarch

Make the passion fruit curd: In a small saucepan, whisk together the passion fruit puree, lemon juice, sugar, salt and egg yolks. Cook over medium-low heat, whisking continuously until the mixture thickens, 10 to 15 minutes. The curd is ready when it can coat the back of a wooden spoon. Once it's done, add the butter and whisk until everything is incorporated and smooth. Strain the curd through a sieve to get rid of any lumps and transfer to a glass jar. Refrigerate for a couple of hours, or until it comes to a spreadable consistency.

Make the meringue: Preheat the oven to 280°F (140°C) or 240°F (120°C) if using a fan-assisted oven. Place the egg whites, sugar and salt in the bowl of a stand mixer (see Notes) and combine with a whisk. Place the bowl over a pot of simmering water, making sure the bowl doesn't touch the water. Heat the egg white mixture, whisking constantly, until the sugar completely dissolves or it reaches 160°F (70°C). This can take up to 5 minutes. You can check whether the sugar is dissolved by rubbing some of the mixture between your fingers.

Carefully transfer the hot bowl to the stand mixer fitted with the whisk attachment. Beat the meringue on high speed until stiff peaks form and it's no longer hot to the touch. Depending on your mixer, this could take up to 10 to 15 minutes. After you've reached the glossy, stiff peak stage, turn off the mixer and add the vanilla, white vinegar and cornstarch. Beat for another 10 to 15 seconds, or until everything is combined.

Draw a 9-inch (23-cm) circle on a piece of parchment paper to use as a guideline. Using a little bit of meringue on the corners, stick the paper to a baking sheet so it doesn't move.

(continued)

Topping

1¼ cups (300 g) heavy cream, cold

1 tbsp (8 g) powdered sugar

½ tsp vanilla extract

10.5 oz (300 g) fresh fruit, or more

Scrape the meringue into the middle of the circle and spread it with an offset palette knife, making sure to stay inside the circle as best you can. Smooth the sides and make a dip in the middle, then pull diagonal lines from bottom to top with an offset palette knife or a spoon, for decorative purposes. Alternatively, you can make rustic swirls or peaks.

Place the meringue in the oven on the middle rack and bake for 60 to 70 minutes. It needs to be crispy on the outside, with just a touch of golden color. When it's done, turn off the oven and leave the meringue inside to cool gradually.

When the meringue is completely cool, carefully place it on a serving plate. In a large bowl, beat the cream with the powdered sugar and vanilla using an electric hand mixer until it forms medium soft peaks. Fill the dip in the meringue with some passion fruit curd and then top it with whipped cream using a spoon. Add some more passion fruit curd over it and top with fresh berries or fresh fruit of your choice.

Serve immediately. Pavlova is best the same day, but you can keep it in an airtight container in the fridge for a couple of days. However, it's possible the sugar will start oozing out from the meringue due to humidity in the fridge.

Notes: When making any kind of meringue, make sure to clean the bowl and the whisk with some vinegar and paper towels to get rid of any possible grease before whipping.

Don't worry about the cracking on the outside of the meringue; it's normal and happens even when you do everything right.

Luscious & Nutty

When I think of autumn (which is coincidentally my favorite season) in terms of food, the first things that come to my mind are the warm, rich flavors of nuts and caramel—hence the title of this chapter. So many bakers get their mojo back the moment colder weather arrives, and I'm definitely one of them.

My favorite way of incorporating nuts into my cakes is by making nut butters. It's such an easy process that gives such a deep flavor because of all the oil releasing than just simply using nuts as they are. Oh, and if you want the best possible flavor, make sure to toast the nuts first.

In this chapter, you'll find candy bar–inspired cakes—such as the Coconut Cream Almond Cake (page 119) and Ferrero Rocher® Hazelnut Cake (page 127), of which I'm incredibly proud—to easy yet nothing short of delicious cakes like Pistachio Orange Cardamom Cake (page 136) and a classic carrot walnut cake (page 146) in sheet form.

And for rich, luscious caramel flavors, don't miss the Caramel Cornflake Cake (page 140), whose cornflake crunch will become your new favorite snack, and the incredible Dulce de Leche Cinnamon Crunch Cake (page 133), which will have you jumping for joy as you bundle up for fall flavors.

Coconut Cream Almond Cake

This one is for all the coconut lovers. The almond coconut butter is one of the best things I've made—it gives exceptional flavor both to the cake and the filling. And that filling, let me tell you—it tastes just like a Raffaello candy bar. Consider it officially approved by Raffaello lovers, including me. Fair warning, you might or might not eat half of this cake on its own, so it would be smart to buy extra ingredients, you know—just in case.

. . . .

Serves 12 to 14

Almond Coconut Butter
7 oz (200 g) blanched almonds

3.5 oz (100 g) unsweetened coconut flakes

1 to 2 tsp (5 to 10 ml) vegetable oil (optional)

Almond Coconut Ganache
3.5 oz (100 g) almond coconut butter

7 oz (200 g) white chocolate, finely chopped

½ cup + 2 tsp (135 g) heavy cream

Coconut Buttercream
¼ cup (30 g) all-purpose flour

Scant ¾ cup (140 g) granulated sugar

Pinch of salt

9 oz (250 g) coconut milk

1 cup (2 sticks; 225 g) unsalted butter, at room temperature

½ tsp vanilla extract

Make the almond coconut butter: In a dry skillet, toast the almonds and coconut flakes over medium-high heat, stirring constantly, until golden brown and aromatic. Remove from the heat and let cool for 10 to 15 minutes. Place the mixture in a food processor and pulse until it starts to look creamy and smooth. If you feel that the processing is taking too long and your food processor might be overheating, add 1 to 2 teaspoons (5 to 10 ml) of vegetable oil to help the mixture get smooth and creamy in an instant. Transfer the butter to a clean jar and keep at room temperature until needed.

Make the ganache: In a medium-sized, heatproof bowl, add the almond coconut butter and the white chocolate. In a small saucepan, bring the cream just barely to a simmer, then pour it over the chocolate. Cover with a plate and let sit for 1 to 2 minutes. Stir with a spatula until combined and smooth. Alternatively, you can do this (using a microwave-safe bowl) in a microwave in 30-second intervals. Cover it with plastic wrap touching the surface and leave it to cool and thicken to a spreadable consistency.

Begin the buttercream: In a small, heavy-bottomed saucepan, whisk together the flour, sugar, salt and coconut milk. Cook over medium to high heat, whisking constantly so the mixture doesn't burn or catch on the bottom of the pan. Once it starts to thicken and you notice bubbling, cook for another 2 minutes, still whisking constantly, until it resembles pastry cream. This whole process could take up to 10 minutes.

When the pudding base is done, strain it through a sieve onto a shallow plate to get rid of any lumps. Cover it with plastic wrap touching the surface to prevent a skin from forming and let it cool to room temperature. You can speed up the process by letting it cool in the fridge, but prior to using, it must be room temperature.

(continued)

Almond Coconut Cake

Cooking spray or butter, for pans

2 cups (250 g) all-purpose flour

2 tsp (10 g) baking powder

½ tsp fine sea salt

¾ cup + 2 tbsp (210 ml) coconut milk, at room temperature

3 tbsp (45 ml) sunflower oil

½ tsp vanilla extract

½ cup (1 stick; 115 g) unsalted butter, at room temperature

1¼ cups (250 g) granulated sugar

3.5 oz (100 g) almond coconut butter

3 large eggs, at room temperature

Make the cake: Preheat the oven to 350°F (175°C) or 325°F (160°C) if using a fan-assisted oven. Grease three 6-inch (15-cm) round cake pans with cooking spray or butter and line the bottoms with parchment paper.

Sift the flour, baking powder and salt into a medium-sized bowl and whisk to combine. In a measuring jug, lightly whisk together the coconut milk, sunflower oil and vanilla.

Using a stand mixer fitted with the paddle attachment, beat the butter with half of the sugar until pale and fluffy, 2 to 3 minutes. Add the rest of the sugar with the almond coconut butter and beat to combine. Add the eggs, one at a time, making sure each is fully incorporated before adding the next.

Next, add the flour mixture in three additions, alternating with the sour cream mixture to avoid splashing and overmixing the batter. After each addition, mix the batter just until combined. Scrape the bowl a couple of times with a silicone spatula to make sure everything is mixed nicely.

Divide the batter equally by weight among the prepared pans and level with an offset palette knife, then bake for 22 to 25 minutes. It's best to check the cakes after 22 minutes and then adjust the baking time accordingly, because ovens can vary. The cakes are done if they spring back when lightly touched and when a skewer inserted into the middle comes out mostly clean. Remove from the oven and leave to cool in their pans on a wire rack for 10 to 15 minutes to firm up a little bit before removing them from the pans to cool completely.

While the cakes are cooling, finish the coconut frosting: Using a stand mixer fitted with the paddle attachment, beat the butter for 5 minutes, or until it's pale and fluffy, then add the previously made pudding base, one spoonful at a time. Beat everything until nicely incorporated with no lumps. Lastly, add the vanilla and beat for a couple of seconds, or until smooth and combined.

Shredded coconut, for decorating (I used roughly 1¼ to 2 cups [100 to 150 g] to cover my cake completely)

Assemble the cake: Start by leveling the tops of your cakes using a cake leveler or a long, serrated knife for a neater look, if needed. Then, put a little bit of buttercream in the middle of a serving plate or cake board to keep the cake from moving around. Place it on a turntable for easier handling and decorating.

Place one cake layer on the serving plate and, using a small, offset palette knife, spread the almond coconut ganache over the top of the cake layer, about ⅜ inch (1 cm) thick. Top it with the next cake layer and repeat the process. Place the final cake layer on top, making sure it's upside down to get a nice, smooth surface on top.

Next, apply a thin layer of ganache around the cake and smooth it using a cake scraper to keep in the crumbs. Chill the cake in the fridge for 30 to 60 minutes. Once the crumb coat is firm, frost the cake with the buttercream and smooth it using a cake scraper. By pressing gently, cover the whole cake with shredded coconut. Put the remaining buttercream in a piping bag fitted with an open star nozzle and pipe dollops on top of the cake.

Keep the cake tightly covered in plastic wrap or in an airtight container at room temperature for 2 days or in the fridge for up to a week. Allow it to come to room temperature before serving.

> **Note:** Use coconut milk that has at least 70 percent coconut, with water as the only additional ingredient. The best kind comes in a carton, but you can use some canned ones, too.

Peanut Butter *Banana* Caramel Cake

This moist banana cake is a longtime family favorite. With its strong, sweet banana flavor, it fits perfectly with the silky, salty peanut butter frosting and salted caramel filling to create a cake truly deserving of a spotlight. For the best flavor, always use overripe, black bananas.

. . . .

Serves 12 to 14

Salted Caramel Sauce

1 cup (200 g) granulated sugar

¼ cup (60 g) water

¾ cup (180 ml) heavy cream

½ tsp vanilla extract

¾ tsp fine sea salt

Peanut Butter Buttercream

⅓ cup (45 g) all-purpose flour

1 cup (200 g) granulated sugar

½ tsp fine sea salt

1½ cups (360 ml) whole milk

1⅓ cups (2⅔ sticks; 300 g) unsalted butter, at room temperature

Rounded ⅓ cup (100 g) smooth peanut butter, at room temperature

½ tsp vanilla extract

Make the salted caramel sauce: In a small, heavy-bottomed saucepan, combine the granulated sugar and water. Make sure every sugar granule is covered with water. Bring to a simmer over medium-high heat and continue to cook until it reaches a golden amber color. Do not stir the mixture under any circumstance, or else it will crystallize. This can take up to 15 minutes, but I suggest keeping an eye on it at all times because caramel burns easily.

Meanwhile, in a separate saucepan, bring the cream and vanilla to a simmer. Once the sugar syrup reaches the desired color, remove it from the heat and pour the cream mixture over the syrup in a slow and steady stream, stirring constantly with a silicone spatula. There will be a lot of bubbles and steam, so be careful not to burn yourself. Once all the bubbles have subsided, put the saucepan back on the stove and cook it for another minute, stirring constantly. When it's done, stir in the salt and transfer the caramel to a clean jar to cool to room temperature.

Begin the buttercream: In a small, heavy-bottomed saucepan, whisk together the flour, granulated sugar, salt and milk. Cook over medium to high heat, whisking constantly so the mixture doesn't burn or catch on the bottom of the pan. Once it starts to thicken and you notice bubbling, cook for another 2 minutes, still whisking constantly, until it resembles pastry cream. This whole process could take up to 10 minutes.

When the pudding base is done, strain it through a sieve onto a shallow plate to get rid of any lumps. Cover it with plastic wrap touching the surface to prevent a skin from forming and let it cool to room temperature. You can speed up the process by letting it cool in the fridge, but prior to using, it must be room temperature.

(continued)

Peanut Butter *Banana* Caramel Cake
(Continued)

. . . .

Banana Cake

Cooking spray or butter, for pans

2 cups (250 g) all-purpose flour

2 tsp (10 g) baking powder

¼ tsp ground cinnamon

½ tsp fine sea salt

3 tbsp (45 ml) whole milk, at room temperature

Rounded ⅔ cup (160 g) sour cream, at room temperature

3 tbsp (45 ml) sunflower oil

½ tsp vanilla extract

½ cup (1 stick; 115 g) unsalted butter, at room temperature

¾ cup (150 g) granulated sugar

⅓ cup + 2 tbsp (100 g) soft light brown sugar

2 large eggs, at room temperature

Rounded ¾ cup (180 g) mashed overripe banana

Roasted salted peanuts, for decorating (optional)

Make the cake: Preheat the oven to 350°F (175°C) or 325°F (160°C) if using a fan-assisted oven. Grease three 6-inch (15-cm) round cake pans with cooking spray or butter and line the bottoms with parchment paper.

Sift the flour, baking powder, cinnamon and salt into a medium-sized bowl and whisk to combine. In a measuring jug, lightly whisk together the milk, sour cream, sunflower oil and vanilla.

Using a stand mixer fitted with the paddle attachment, beat the butter with the granulated sugar until pale and fluffy, 2 to 3 minutes. Add the brown sugar and beat to combine. Add the eggs, one at a time, making sure each is fully incorporated before adding the next. Add the mashed banana and mix until combined.

Next, add the flour mixture in three additions, alternating with the sour cream mixture to avoid splashing and overmixing the batter. After each addition, mix the batter just until combined. Scrape the bowl a couple of times with a silicone spatula to make sure everything is mixed nicely.

Divide the batter equally by weight among the prepared pans and level with an offset palette knife. Bake for 22 to 25 minutes. It's best to check the cakes after 22 minutes and then adjust the baking time accordingly, because ovens can vary. The cakes are done if they spring back when lightly touched and when a skewer inserted into the middle comes out mostly clean. Remove from the oven and leave them to cool in their pans on a wire rack for 10 to 15 minutes to firm up a little bit before removing them from the pans to cool completely.

While the cakes are cooling, finish the buttercream: Using the stand mixer fitted with the paddle attachment, beat the butter for 5 minutes, or until it's pale and fluffy. Add the peanut butter and beat until combined. Scrape the bowl with a spatula occasionally to make sure everything is thoroughly combined, then add the previously made pudding base, one spoonful at a time. Beat everything until nicely incorporated with no lumps. Lastly, add the vanilla and beat for a couple of seconds, or until smooth and combined.

Assemble the cake: Start by leveling the tops of your cakes using a cake leveler or a long, serrated knife for a neater look, if needed. Then, put a little bit of buttercream in the middle of a serving plate or cake board to keep the cake from moving around. Place it on a turntable for easier handling and decorating.

Place one cake layer on the serving plate and, using a small, offset palette knife or a piping bag filled with buttercream, spread the frosting over the top of the cake layer, about ⅜ inch (1 cm) thick. Make a dam around it and fill with a couple of tablespoons (about 30 ml) of salted caramel sauce. Top it with the next cake layer and repeat the process. Place the final cake layer on top, making sure it's upside down to get a nice, smooth surface on top.

Next, apply a thin layer of frosting around the cake and smooth it using a cake scraper to keep in the crumbs. Chill the cake in the fridge for 30 to 60 minutes before applying the final coat of frosting and decorating.

Once the crumb coat is firm, frost the cake with the remaining buttercream. Smooth the sides and the top using a cake scraper and an offset palette knife. Then, dab some of the leftover caramel sauce on the sides of the cake using an offset palette knife, and make caramel swirls on top of the cake. You can pipe buttercream dollops on top of the cake as well. If desired, sprinkle some chopped roasted, salted peanuts on top.

Keep the cake tightly covered in plastic wrap or in an airtight container at room temperature for 2 days or in the fridge for up to a week. Allow it to come to room temperature before serving.

Note: You can also decorate the cake with peanut brittle (page 24).

Ferrero Rocher® *Hazelnut* Cake

This was one of the first recipes I developed and truly loved. I've improved and changed a couple of things with this version, but it's still the same cake that made my inbox full of order requests all those years ago. The hazelnut meringue brings that crunchy element of Ferrero Rocher, while the hazelnut butter ganache gives Nutella a run for its money. The chocolate hazelnut flavor is also present in the soft, moist cake layers, and the whole cake is covered in silky chocolate buttercream. If you try only one recipe from this book, I won't be mad if it's this one.

. . . .

Serves 12 to 14

Hazelnut Butter
10.5 oz (300 g) blanched chopped hazelnuts

1 to 2 tsp (5 to 10 ml) vegetable oil (optional)

Chocolate Buttercream
¼ cup (30 g) all-purpose flour

⅔ cup (130 g) granulated sugar

Pinch of salt

1 cup + 2 tsp (250 ml) whole milk

1 cup (2 sticks; 225 g) unsalted butter, at room temperature

5.5 oz (150 g) good-quality 55% dark chocolate, melted

½ tsp vanilla extract

Meringue Crunch
⅓ cup (80 g) egg whites (about 2 large eggs)

Pinch of salt

5 tbsp + 2 tsp (70 g) superfine sugar

3 tbsp (20 g) unsweetened cocoa powder

Scant 2 oz (50 g) finely chopped hazelnuts

Make the hazelnut butter: In a dry skillet over medium-high heat, toast the hazelnuts, stirring constantly, until golden. Remove from the heat and let cool for 10 to 15 minutes. Transfer them to a food processor and pulse until the hazelnut butter starts to look creamy and smooth. If you feel that the processing is taking too long and your food processor might be overheating, add 1 to 2 teaspoons (5 to 10 ml) of vegetable oil to help the hazelnut butter get smooth and creamy in an instant. Transfer to a clean jar and keep at room temperature until needed.

Begin the buttercream: In a small, heavy-bottomed saucepan, whisk together the flour, granulated sugar, salt and milk. Cook over medium to high heat, whisking constantly so the mixture doesn't burn or catch on the bottom of the pan. Once it starts to thicken and you notice bubbling, cook for another 2 minutes, still whisking constantly, until it resembles pastry cream. This whole process could take up to 10 minutes.

When the pudding base is done, strain it through a sieve onto a shallow plate to get rid of any possible lumps. Cover it with plastic wrap touching the surface to prevent a skin from forming and let it cool to room temperature. You can speed up the process by letting it cool in the fridge, but prior to using, it must be room temperature.

Make the meringue crunch: Preheat the oven to 250°F (120°C) or 220°F (105°C) if using a fan-assisted oven. Line a 9 x 13–inch (23 x 33–cm) rimmed baking sheet with parchment paper.

Using a stand mixer fitted with the whisk attachment, beat the egg whites with a pinch of salt on high speed until soft peaks form. Reduce the speed to medium-low and with the mixer still going, add the superfine sugar, one spoonful at a time. Once all the sugar is added, beat on high speed until the sugar is completely dissolved and stiff peaks form. Using a tiny bit of the meringue on the corners, stick the parchment paper to a baking sheet so it doesn't move.

Using a spatula, carefully fold in the cocoa powder and hazelnuts, until fully combined. Spread the meringue over the baking sheet as evenly as possible and bake for 60 to 90 minutes, or until fully baked and crunchy on the outside. When it's done, remove from the oven and let it cool in the pan until needed.

(continued)

Milk Chocolate Hazelnut Filling

3.5 oz (100 g) hazelnut butter

7 oz (200 g) 33% milk chocolate, finely chopped

½ cup + 2 tsp (135 g) heavy cream

Chocolate Hazelnut Cake

Cooking spray or butter, for pans

1⅔ cups (200 g) all-purpose flour

2 tsp (10 g) baking powder

Rounded ¼ cup (30 g) unsweetened cocoa powder

½ tsp fine sea salt

Rounded ¾ cup (180 g) sour cream, at room temperature

¼ cup (60 ml) whole milk, at room temperature

3 tbsp (45 ml) sunflower oil

1 tsp vanilla extract

½ cup (1 stick; 115 g) unsalted butter, at room temperature

1¼ cups (250 g) granulated sugar

3.5 oz (100 g) hazelnut butter

3 large eggs, at room temperature

Make the milk chocolate hazelnut filling: In a medium-sized, heatproof bowl, combine the hazelnut butter and milk chocolate. In a small saucepan, bring the cream just barely to a simmer and pour it over the chocolate. Cover with a plate and let sit for 1 to 2 minutes. Stir with a spatula until combined and smooth. Alternatively, you can do this (using a microwave-safe bowl) in a microwave in 30-second intervals. Cover it with a piece of plastic wrap touching the surface and leave to cool and thicken to a spreadable consistency.

Make the cake: Preheat the oven to 350°F (175°C) or 325°F (160°C) if using a fan-assisted oven. Grease three 6-inch (15-cm) round cake pans with cooking spray or butter and line the bottoms with parchment paper.

Sift the flour, baking powder, cocoa powder and salt into a medium-sized bowl and whisk to combine. In a measuring jug, lightly whisk together the sour cream, milk, sunflower oil and vanilla.

Using a stand mixer fitted with the paddle attachment or an electric hand mixer, beat the butter with half the granulated sugar until pale and fluffy, 2 to 3 minutes. Add the rest of the granulated sugar along with the hazelnut butter and beat to combine. Add the eggs, one at a time, making sure each is fully incorporated before adding the next.

Next, add the flour mixture to the butter mixture in three additions, alternating with the sour cream mixture to avoid splashing and overmixing the batter. After each addition, mix the batter just until combined. Scrape the bowl a couple of times with a silicone spatula to make sure everything is mixed nicely.

Divide the batter equally by weight among the prepared pans and level it with an offset palette knife. Bake for 22 to 25 minutes. It's best to check the cakes after 22 minutes and then adjust the baking time accordingly, because ovens can vary. The cakes are done when they're springy on the top and when a skewer inserted into the middle comes out mostly clean. Remove from the oven and leave them to cool in their pans on a wire rack for 10 to 15 minutes to firm up a little bit before inverting them from the pans onto a wire rack to cool completely.

While the cakes are cooling, finish the buttercream: Using a stand mixer fitted with the paddle attachment, beat the butter for 5 minutes, or until it's pale and fluffy, then add the previously made pudding base, one spoonful at a time. Beat everything until nicely incorporated with no lumps. Lastly, add the melted chocolate and vanilla and beat until smooth and combined.

Chocolate Ganache

2 oz (60 g) 55% dark chocolate, finely chopped

⅓ cup (70 g) heavy cream

Finely chopped hazelnuts, Ferrero Rochers and whole hazelnuts, for decorating (optional)

Assemble the cake: Start by leveling the tops of your cakes using a cake leveler or a long, serrated knife for a neater look, if needed. Then, put a little bit of buttercream in the middle of a serving plate or your cake board to keep the cake from moving around. Place it on a turntable for easier handling and decorating.

Place one cake layer on the serving plate and using a small, offset palette knife or a piping bag filled with chocolate hazelnut ganache, spread a layer of filling over the top of the cake, about ⅜ inch (1 cm) thick and sprinkle with crushed meringue pieces. Top it with the next cake layer and repeat the process. Place the final cake layer on top, making sure it's upside down to get a nice, smooth surface on top.

Next, apply a thin layer of frosting around the cake and smooth it using a cake scraper to keep in the crumbs. Chill the cake in the fridge for 30 to 60 minutes before applying the final coat of frosting and decorating.

Once the crumb coat is firm, frost the cake with the chocolate buttercream. Smooth the sides and the top using a cake scraper and an offset palette knife. Gently press the finely chopped hazelnuts (if using) onto the sides of the cake in an uneven layer, starting at the bottom and working about a quarter to a third of the way up. Place the cake in the fridge for 30 minutes before final decorations.

Make the chocolate ganache: Place the chocolate in a small, heatproof bowl. In a small saucepan, bring the cream to a simmer, then pour it over the chocolate. Cover with a plate and let sit for 1 to 2 minutes, or until the chocolate softens and begins to melt. Stir with a spatula until combined and smooth. Alternatively, you can do this (using a microwave-safe bowl) in a microwave in 30-second intervals. If it seems too loose, leave it to cool and thicken for 10 to 15 minutes before pouring over the chilled cake.

When your cake is chilled and you're ready to decorate, pour two-thirds of the chocolate ganache onto the middle of your cake and slowly spread it around with a small offset palette knife for a natural-looking drip. If you need more, add the remaining third of the ganache on top and spread it in the same manner. You might end up with a little leftover ganache.

Put the cake in the fridge so the chocolate drip has time to set. Decorate the top with any leftover buttercream and Ferrero Rochers or hazelnuts, if desired.

Keep the cake tightly covered in plastic wrap or in an airtight container at room temperature for 2 days or in the fridge for up to a week. Allow it to come to room temperature before serving.

Sour Cherry Almond Cake

Sour cherries are one of my favorite ingredients in desserts. Cherry strudel? Count me in. Naturally, that soft strudel filling had to sneak its way into this book, and the vanilla frosting featured here is reminiscent of the scoop of vanilla ice cream I'd put on a warm piece of strudel.

Serves 12 to 14

Sour Cherry Pie Filling

7 oz (200 g) frozen sour cherries

Rounded ⅓ cup (80 g) granulated sugar

1 tbsp (8 g) cornstarch

1 tbsp (15 ml) water

Vanilla Buttercream

Scant ½ cup (55 g) all-purpose flour

Rounded cup (225 g) granulated sugar

½ tsp fine sea salt

Scant 1¾ cups (390 ml) whole milk

1½ cups + 2 tsp (3 sticks + 2 tsp; 350 g) unsalted butter, at room temperature

2 tsp (10 ml) vanilla extract

Burgundy gel food coloring

Almond Cake

Cooking spray or butter, for pans

2 cups (250 g) all-purpose flour

2 tsp (10 g) baking powder

¼ tsp baking soda

¼ tsp ground cinnamon

½ tsp fine sea salt

4.5 oz (120 g) finely chopped almonds, toasted

¼ cup (60 ml) whole milk, at room temperature

Rounded ¾ cup (180 g) sour cream, at room temperature

½ tsp vanilla extract

⅔ cup (1⅓ sticks; 150 g) unsalted butter, at room temperature

Rounded cup (250 g) soft light brown sugar

3 large eggs, at room temperature

Make the sour cherry pie filling: In a small, heavy-bottomed saucepan, bring the frozen cherries and sugar to a boil over medium heat. Simmer for a few minutes, or until the cherries release all their juices. Meanwhile, in a small bowl, dilute the cornstarch with the water and pour the mixture over the cherries, mixing constantly with a large wooden spoon until everything is incorporated.

Bring the mixture to a boil and cook for a few minutes, or until the filling becomes gloopy and thick. If the filling is too thick, you can always add a splash of water. Once thickened, transfer the filling to a bowl and cover with plastic wrap touching the surface to prevent a skin from forming. Leave at room temperature or in the fridge to cool completely.

Begin the buttercream: In a small, heavy-bottomed saucepan, whisk together the flour, sugar, salt and milk. Cook over medium to high heat, whisking constantly so the mixture doesn't burn or catch on the bottom of the pan. Once it starts to thicken and you notice bubbling, cook for another 2 minutes, still whisking constantly, until it resembles pastry cream. This whole process could take up to 10 minutes.

When the pudding base is done, strain it through a sieve onto a shallow plate to get rid of any lumps. Cover it with plastic wrap touching the surface to prevent a skin from forming and let it cool to room temperature. You can speed up the process by letting it cool in the fridge, but prior to using, it must be room temperature.

Make the cake: Preheat the oven to 350°F (175°C) or 325°F (160°C) if using a fan-assisted oven. Grease three 6-inch (15-cm) round cake pans with cooking spray or butter and line the bottoms with parchment paper.

Sift the flour, baking powder, baking soda, cinnamon and salt into a medium-sized bowl. Add the toasted almonds and whisk together. In a measuring jug, lightly whisk together the milk, sour cream and vanilla.

Using a stand mixer fitted with the paddle attachment or an electric hand mixer, beat the butter with half of the brown sugar until pale and fluffy, 2 to 3 minutes. Add the rest of the brown sugar and beat to combine. Add the eggs, one at a time, making sure each is fully incorporated before adding the next.

(continued)

Next, add the flour mixture to the butter mixture in three additions, alternating with the sour cream mixture to avoid splashing and overmixing the batter. After each addition, mix the batter just until combined. Scrape the bowl a couple of times with a silicone spatula to make sure everything is mixed nicely.

Divide the batter equally by weight among the prepared pans and level it with an offset palette knife. Bake for 22 to 25 minutes. It's best to check the cakes after 22 minutes and then adjust the baking time accordingly, because ovens can vary. The cakes are done when they're springy on the top and when a skewer inserted into the middle comes out mostly clean. Remove from the oven and leave them to cool in their pans on a wire rack for 10 to 15 minutes to firm up a little bit before inverting them from the pans onto the wire rack to cool completely.

While the cakes are cooling, finish the buttercream: Using a stand mixer fitted with the paddle attachment, beat the butter for 5 minutes, until it's pale and fluffy, then add the previously made pudding base, one spoonful at a time. Beat everything until nicely incorporated with no lumps. Lastly, add the vanilla and beat for a couple of seconds, or until smooth and combined.

Assemble the cake: Start by leveling the tops of your cakes using a cake leveler or a long, serrated knife for a neater look, if needed. Then, put a little bit of buttercream in the middle of a serving plate or your cake board to keep the cake from moving around. Place it on a turntable for easier handling and decorating.

Place one cake layer on the serving plate and, using a small, offset palette knife or a piping bag filled with buttercream, spread the frosting over the top of the cake layer, about ¼ inch (6 mm) thick. Make a dam around the edges and fill with cherries. Top it with the next cake layer and repeat the process. Place the final cake layer on top, making sure it's upside down to get a nice, smooth surface on top.

Next, apply a thin layer of frosting around the cake and smooth it using a cake scraper to keep in the crumbs. Chill the cake in the fridge for 30 to 60 minutes before applying the final coat of frosting and decorating.

Transferring it first to three separate bowls, tint half of the remaining frosting with some burgundy gel food coloring in three shades. Make buttercream flowers by individually piping them onto small pieces of parchment paper using a petal nozzle. Place them on a baking sheet and freeze until needed.

Once the crumb coat is firm, frost the cake with the remaining buttercream and smooth it using a cake scraper. Place the frozen buttercream flowers in a curved shape starting at the top of the cake.

Keep the cake tightly covered in plastic wrap or in an airtight container at room temperature for 2 days or in the fridge for up to a week. Allow it to come to room temperature before serving.

Dulce de Leche **Cinnamon Crunch Cake**

Originating in Argentina but made across the whole of Latin America, dulce de leche is a sweet milk spread that is essentially caramelized milk and sugar . . . and tastes absolutely amazing. I personally find that it reaches its full potential when combined with cinnamon, so pairing it with a spicy cinnamon cake in this recipe was the perfect choice. The easy buttercream frosting is an adaptation of sweetened condensed milk buttercream, also known as Russian buttercream. It's not overly sweet, and it has a beautiful, silky texture that doesn't crust.

Serves 12 to 14

Dulce de Leche
4¼ cups (1 L) whole milk

1½ cups (300 g) granulated sugar

¼ tsp baking soda

½ tsp ground cinnamon

Cinnamon Cake
Cooking spray or butter, for pans

2 cups (250 g) all-purpose flour

2 tsp (10 g) baking powder

1½ tsp (3 g) ground cinnamon

½ tsp salt

¼ cup (60 ml) whole milk, at room temperature

Rounded ¾ cup (180 g) sour cream, at room temperature

3 tbsp (45 ml) sunflower oil

1 tsp vanilla extract

½ cup (1 stick; 115 g) unsalted butter, at room temperature

Rounded cup (250 g) soft light brown sugar

3 large eggs, at room temperature

Make the dulce de leche: In a large, heavy-bottomed saucepan, whisk together the milk, granulated sugar, baking soda and cinnamon. Bring the mixture to a boil over medium-high heat. Make sure not to take your eyes off of it, otherwise it might erupt all over your stove.

Once the mixture reaches a boiling point, remove the foam with a spoon, lower the heat to low and let it simmer, uncovered, for about 90 minutes, stirring occasionally. Once it starts to thicken, stir it more frequently to prevent burning. Cook until it becomes a dark caramel color and looks like a thick caramel sauce, though it will thicken more once cooled. When it's done, transfer it to a jar and let it cool completely until needed.

Make the cake: Preheat the oven to 350°F (175°C) or 325°F (160°C) if using a fan-assisted oven. Grease three 6-inch (15-cm) round cake pans with cooking spray or butter and line the bottoms with parchment paper.

Sift the flour, baking powder, cinnamon and salt into a medium-sized bowl and whisk to combine. In a measuring jug, lightly whisk together the milk, sour cream, sunflower oil and vanilla.

Using a stand mixer fitted with the paddle attachment, beat the butter with half of the sugar until pale and fluffy, 2 to 3 minutes. Add the rest of the sugar and beat to combine. Add the eggs, one at a time, making sure each is fully incorporated before adding the next.

Next, add the flour mixture in three additions, alternating with the sour cream mixture to avoid splashing and overmixing the batter. After each addition, mix the batter just until combined. Scrape the bowl a couple of times with a silicone spatula to make sure everything is mixed nicely.

Divide the batter equally by weight among the prepared pans and level it with an offset palette knife, then bake for 22 to 25 minutes. It's best to check the cakes after 22 minutes and then adjust the baking time accordingly, because ovens can vary. The cakes are done when they're springy on the top and when a skewer inserted into the middle comes out mostly clean. When they're done, remove them from the oven and leave them to cool in their pans on a wire rack for 10 to 15 minutes to firm up a little bit before removing them from the pans to cool completely.

(continued)

Dulce de Leche **Cinnamon Crunch Cake**
(Continued)

. . . .

Cinnamon Streusel Crunch

Scant ¾ cup (90 g) all-purpose flour

1 tsp ground cinnamon

Pinch of salt

Scant ⅓ cup (70 g) soft light brown sugar

¼ cup + 1 tsp (½ stick + 1 tsp; 60 g) unsalted butter, melted

1 large egg white, whisked

Dulce de Leche Buttercream

1½ cups + 2 tbsp (3 sticks + 2 tbsp; 375 g) unsalted butter, at room temperature

1½ cups (300 g) dulce de leche

Pinch of salt

Notes: If you have your favorite brand of dulce de leche, feel free to use that instead of making your own. The homemade version will last for a couple of weeks in the fridge.

For a semi-homemade dulce de leche, you can boil an unopened can of sweetened condensed milk, uncovered, for 3 to 4 hours, making sure there's always water at least 2 to 3 inches (5 to 8 cm) above the can. When it's done, carefully take it out, place on a wire rack and leave to cool completely before trying to open it, because it will be very hot and under pressure.

Make the cinnamon streusel crunch: Sift and combine the flour, cinnamon, salt and brown sugar in a small bowl. Gradually add the melted butter, while stirring with the fork, until the mixture starts clumping together. Add the whisked egg white and stir to combine. Put in the fridge to firm up a little bit.

Preheat the oven to 375°F (190°C) or 350°F (175°C) for a fan-assisted oven. Sprinkle the streusel over a rimmed baking sheet lined with parchment paper. Bake for 20 to 25 minutes, or until golden brown.

Make the buttercream: Using a stand mixer fitted with the paddle attachment, beat the butter for 5 to 10 minutes, or until it's pale and fluffy. Add the dulce de leche along with the salt and beat at medium-high speed until fully incorporated. Scrape the bowl with a silicone spatula a couple of times to make sure everything is mixed nicely.

Assemble the cake: Start by leveling the tops of your cakes using a cake leveler or a long, serrated knife for a neater look, if needed. Then, put a little bit of buttercream in the middle of a serving plate or your cake board to keep the cake from moving around. Place it on a turntable for easier handling and decorating.

Place 1 cake layer on the serving plate and, using a small, offset palette knife or a piping bag filled with buttercream, spread the frosting over the top of the cake layer, about ⅜ inch (1 cm) thick. Make a dam around it and fill with a couple of tablespoons (about 30 ml) of dulce de leche and sprinkle some cinnamon streusel crunch over it. Top it with the next cake layer and repeat the process. Place the final cake layer on top, making sure it's upside down to get a nice, smooth surface on top.

Next, apply a thin layer of frosting around the cake and smooth it using a cake scraper to keep in the crumbs. Chill the cake in the fridge for 30 to 60 minutes. Once the crumb coat is firm, frost the cake with the remaining buttercream in a rustic manner and decorate the top with the cinnamon streusel crunch.

The cake is best when served and eaten at room temperature. You can keep the cake in the fridge, covered in plastic wrap or in an airtight container, but take it out of the fridge at least an hour before serving.

Pistachio Orange Cardamom Cake

I'll never forget the first time I tried cardamom. Oh, my goodness, I knew right at that moment that I'd met my favorite spice. It's been more than ten years now since that moment, and cardamom proudly holds the top spice position in my life. With its spicy yet incredibly refreshing and citrusy aromas, cardamom is the perfect pairing for oranges as well as nuts—with pistachios being a personal favorite. This incredibly flavorful and moist cake is the perfect choice any day of the week because it comes together so easily. Instead of oranges, you can use mandarins, clementines or even lemons—they all go very well with cardamom and pistachio.

· ·

Serves 10 to 12

Cake

Cooking spray or butter, for pan

2 oranges

5 tbsp (70 g) granulated sugar

2 tsp (4 g) ground cardamom, divided

Scant 1¼ cups (150 g) all-purpose flour

1¾ tsp (9 g) baking powder

½ tsp fine sea salt (if not using salted pistachios)

3.5 oz (100 g) finely ground salted and roasted pistachios

Rounded ½ cup (120 g) sour cream, at room temperature

3 tbsp (45 ml) sunflower oil

¼ cup (60 ml) whole milk, at room temperature

Finely grated zest of 1 orange

½ tsp vanilla extract

6 tbsp (¾ stick; 90 g) unsalted butter, at room temperature

¾ cup (170 g) soft light brown sugar

2 large eggs, at room temperature

Preheat the oven to 350°F (175°C) or 325°F (160°C) if using a fan-assisted oven. Grease with cooking spray or butter and line with parchment paper a 9-inch (23-cm) round springform pan.

Leaving them unpeeled, cut the oranges into thin slices, discarding the ends. In a small bowl, whisk together the granulated sugar and ½ teaspoon of the ground cardamom until the sugar is evenly coated. Sprinkle 3 tablespoons (40 g) of the spiced sugar on the bottom of the pan and cover with the orange slices. Let the orange slices slightly overlap one another, because they will shrink in the oven. Sprinkle the rest of the spiced sugar over the oranges.

Make the cake: Sift the flour, baking powder, remaining 1½ teaspoons (3 g) of ground cardamom and the salt (if using) into a medium-sized bowl. Add the pistachios and whisk to combine. In a measuring jug, lightly whisk together the sour cream, sunflower oil, milk, orange zest and vanilla.

In a large bowl, using an electric hand mixer, beat the butter and brown sugar for 2 to 3 minutes on medium-high speed, or until it turns pale and fluffy. Add the eggs, one at a time, making sure each is fully combined before adding the next. Scrape the bowl a couple of times with a silicone spatula to make sure everything is mixed nicely.

Next, add the flour mixture to the butter mixture in two additions, alternating with the sour cream mixture. After each addition, beat just until everything is incorporated to avoid overmixing the batter. Scrape the batter gently over the oranges and spread evenly.

Bake for 40 to 45 minutes. The cake is done when it's springy on the top and when a skewer inserted into the middle comes out mostly clean. Once the cake is done, remove from the oven, place it on a wire rack and let it cool in the pan for about 15 minutes before inverting onto a serving plate to cool completely.

The cake is best when served the same day and still just slightly warm. You can keep the cake in the fridge for several days, covered in plastic wrap or in an airtight container, but take it out of the fridge at least an hour before serving.

Pecan *Pear* Honey Loaf Cake

This simple loaf cake is the perfect way to kick off the autumn season. Although apple mostly gets all the glory in the fall, delicate and sweet pear shines in this honey-based cake with the addition of crunchy pecans. If you don't like honey, I have to tell you that this cake was approved even by people who don't like honey on its own—including me. However, if you don't want to take any chances, you can use an additional ½ cup (100 g) of granulated sugar instead and omit the baking soda. Keep in mind, though, that the cake will lose some of its signature flavor.

. . . .

Serves 12 to 14

Cake

Cooking spray or butter, for pan

2 cups (250 g) all-purpose flour

2 tsp (10 g) baking powder

¼ tsp baking soda

½ tsp fine sea salt

4.5 oz (125 g) chopped pecans, toasted

Rounded ¾ cup (180 g) sour cream, at room temperature

¼ cup (85 g) honey

½ tsp vanilla extract

½ cup (1 stick; 115 g) unsalted butter, at room temperature

½ cup (100 g) granulated sugar

3 large eggs, at room temperature

2 cups (300 g) peeled and chopped pears

Powdered sugar, for dusting (optional)

Preheat the oven to 350°F (175°C) or 325°F (160°C) if using a fan-assisted oven. Grease a 9 x 5-inch (23 x 13–cm) loaf pan with cooking spray or butter and line it with parchment paper overhanging the two longer sides for easier handling later.

Make the cake: Sift the flour, baking powder, baking soda and salt into the bowl of a stand mixer, or a medium-sized bowl if you're using an electric hand mixer. Add the toasted pecans and whisk together. In a measuring jug, lightly whisk together the sour cream, honey and vanilla.

Using a stand mixer fitted with the paddle attachment or a separate bowl with an electric hand mixer, beat the butter with the sugar until pale and fluffy, 2 to 3 minutes. Add the eggs, one at a time, making sure each is fully incorporated before adding the next.

Next, add the flour mixture to the butter mixture in three additions, alternating with the sour cream mixture to avoid splashing and overmixing the batter. After each addition, mix the batter just until combined. Scrape the bowl a couple of times with a silicone spatula to make sure everything is mixed nicely.

Lastly, gently fold in the chopped pears and pour the batter into the prepared loaf pan. Bake for 40 to 50 minutes, or until a skewer inserted into the middle comes out mostly clean. Remove it from the oven and let it cool in the pan for 15 to 20 minutes before transferring onto a wire rack to cool completely.

If desired, dust with powdered sugar before serving.

Keep the cake in an airtight container at room temperature for 2 to 3 days or for up to a week in the fridge.

Note: To add a classic sugar icing on top, see the directions for the glaze (leaving out the rosewater) of the Raspberry Rose Loaf Cake (page 66).

Caramel Cornflake Cake

I'm one of those people who can snack on dry cornflakes or eat a bowl for dinner. Although I love plain cornflakes, I can't resist the ones with added flavor, such as honey caramel and nuts. So, I just knew a caramel and cornflake cake had to happen in this book. Inspired by Milk Bar's cereal milk and other cornflake desserts, I infused the milk with cornflakes and added it both to the frosting and the cake layers, for maximum effect. The salted caramel filling ties it all together into a rich, delicious ode to that classic malty cornflake flavor—trust me, you don't want to miss this one!

· ·

Serves 12 to 14

Cornflake Crunch

8 cups (300 g) cornflakes

Rounded ⅓ cup (75 g) granulated sugar

1½ tsp (9 g) fine sea salt

½ cup + 2 tbsp (1 stick + 2 tbsp; 140 g) unsalted butter, melted and cooled

Cornflake-Infused Milk

7 oz (200 g) cornflake crunch

3½ cups (840 ml) whole milk, warm

Salted Caramel Sauce

1 cup (200 g) granulated sugar

¼ cup (60 g) water

¾ cup (180 ml) heavy cream

½ tsp vanilla extract

¾ tsp fine sea salt

Make the cornflake crunch: Preheat the oven to 340°F (170°C) or 300°F (150°C) if using a fan-assisted oven.

Place the cornflakes in a large bowl and, using your hands, crush them into smaller pieces. Add the granulated sugar and salt and toss to combine. Next, add the cooled melted butter and stir with a silicone spatula until evenly coated. Scatter the cornflakes on a rimmed baking sheet lined with parchment paper. Bake for 15 to 20 minutes, or until they look toasted and crunchy. Remove from the oven and allow the cornflakes to cool completely before using.

Make the cornflake-infused milk: Place the cornflake crunch in a large measuring jug. Pour the warmed milk on top and give it a quick stir. Leave to infuse for at least 20 to 30 minutes at room temperature.

When it's ready, strain the mixture through a fine-mesh sieve into a medium-sized bowl. Using the back of a spoon, gently press the cornflakes into the sieve to extract more milk. Be careful not to press too hard so that the mushy cornflakes don't go through. Set aside until needed for the buttercream and cake.

Make the salted caramel sauce: In a small, heavy-bottomed saucepan, combine the granulated sugar and water. Make sure every sugar granule is covered with water. Bring to a simmer over medium-high heat and continue to cook until it reaches a golden amber color. Do not stir the mixture under any circumstance, or else it will crystallize. This can take up to 15 minutes, but I suggest keeping an eye on it at all times, because caramel burns easily.

Meanwhile, in a small saucepan, bring the cream and vanilla to a simmer. Once the sugar syrup reaches the desired color, remove its saucepan from the heat and pour the cream over it in a slow and steady stream, stirring constantly with a silicone spatula. There will be a lot of bubbles and steam, so be careful not to burn yourself.

Once all the bubbles have subsided, put the saucepan of caramel back on the stove and cook it for 1 to 2 minutes, stirring constantly. When it's done, stir in the salt and store in a clean jar to cool to room temperature.

Caramel **Cornflake Cake** (Continued)

(continued)

Cornflake Buttercream

⅓ cup (45 g) all-purpose flour

1 cup (200 g) granulated sugar

¼ tsp fine sea salt

1½ cups (360 ml) cornflake-infused milk

1⅓ cups (2⅔ sticks; 300 g) unsalted butter, at room temperature

Caramel Cornflake Cake

Cooking spray or butter, for pans

2 cups (250 g) all-purpose flour

2 tsp (10 g) baking powder

½ tsp fine sea salt

¾ cup (180 ml) cornflake-infused milk

2 tbsp (30 g) sour cream, at room temperature

3 tbsp (45 ml) sunflower oil

½ tsp vanilla extract

½ cup (1 stick; 115 g) unsalted butter

1 cup (200 g) granulated sugar

3⅓ tbsp (50 g) soft light brown sugar

3 large eggs, at room temperature

2.5 oz (75 g) cornflake crunch

Begin the buttercream: In a small, heavy-bottomed saucepan, whisk together the flour, granulated sugar, salt and cornflake-infused milk. Cook over medium to high heat, whisking constantly so the mixture doesn't burn or catch on the bottom of the pan. Once it starts to thicken and you notice bubbling, cook for another 2 minutes, still whisking constantly, until it resembles pastry cream. This whole process could take up to 10 minutes.

When the pudding base is done, strain it through a sieve onto a shallow plate to get rid of any lumps. Cover it with plastic wrap touching the surface to prevent a skin from forming and let it cool to room temperature. You can speed up the process by letting it cool in the fridge, but prior to using, it must be room temperature.

Make the cake: Preheat the oven to 350°F (175°C) or 325°F (160°C) if using a fan-assisted oven. Grease three 6-inch (15-cm) round cake pans with cooking spray or butter and line the bottoms with parchment paper.

Sift the flour, baking powder and salt into a medium-sized bowl and whisk to combine. In a measuring jug, lightly whisk together the cornflake-infused milk, sour cream, sunflower oil and vanilla.

Using a stand mixer fitted with the paddle attachment, beat the butter with half of the granulated sugar until pale and fluffy, 2 to 3 minutes. Add the rest of the sugar and the brown sugar and beat to combine. Add the eggs, one at a time, making sure each is fully incorporated before adding the next.

Next, add the flour mixture in three additions, alternating with the sour cream mixture to avoid splashing and overmixing the batter. After each addition, mix the batter just until combined. Scrape the bowl a couple of times with a silicone spatula to make sure everything is mixed nicely. Lastly, fold in the cornflake crunch using a silicone spatula.

Divide the batter equally by weight among the prepared pans and level it with an offset palette knife. Bake for 22 to 25 minutes. It's best to check the cakes after 22 minutes and then adjust the baking time accordingly, because ovens can vary. The cakes are done when they're springy on the top and when a skewer inserted into the middle comes out mostly clean. When they're done, remove them from the oven and leave them to cool in their pans on a wire rack for 10 to 15 minutes to firm up a little bit before removing them from the pans to cool completely.

While the cakes are cooling, finish the buttercream: Using the stand mixer fitted with the paddle attachment, beat the butter for 5 minutes, or until it's pale and fluffy, then add the previously made pudding base, one spoonful at a time. Beat everything until nicely incorporated with no lumps.

Assemble the cake: Start by leveling the tops of your cakes using a cake leveler or a long, serrated knife for a neater look, if needed. Then, put a little bit of buttercream in the middle of a serving plate or your cake board to keep the cake from moving around. Place it on a turntable for easier handling and decorating.

Place one cake layer on the serving plate and, using a small, offset palette knife or a piping bag filled with buttercream, spread the frosting over the top of the cake layer, about ⅜ inch (1 cm) thick. Make a dam around it and fill with a couple of tablespoons (about 30 ml) of salted caramel sauce. Sprinkle some of the cornflake crunch over it. Top it with the next cake layer and repeat the process. Place the final cake layer on top, making sure it's upside down to get a nice, smooth surface on top.

Next, apply a thin layer of frosting around the cake and smooth it using a cake scraper to keep in the crumbs. Chill the cake in the fridge for 30 to 60 minutes before applying the final coat of frosting and decorating.

Once the crumb coat is firm, frost the cake with the remaining buttercream, saving a little for the dollops on top. Smooth the sides and the top using a cake scraper and an offset palette knife. Gently press the remaining cornflake crunch onto the sides of the cake in an uneven layer, starting at the bottom.

Chill the cake for 30 to 60 minutes, or until firm to the touch. Cover the top with salted caramel and buttercream dollops.

Keep the cake tightly covered in plastic wrap or in an airtight container at room temperature for 2 days or in the fridge for up to a week. Allow it to come to room temperature before serving.

Lemon Hazelnut Cake

Each season deserves at least one no-fuss, delicious, easy cake, and my pick for autumn is this cake. The combination of toasty, earthy hazelnuts and sharp, fresh lemon with the creaminess of the white chocolate cream cheese frosting is pure comfort, especially when paired with a cup of hot tea.

. . . .

Serves 10 to 12

Cake
Cooking spray or butter, for pan

Scant 1¼ cups (150 g) all-purpose flour

1¾ tsp (8.5 g) baking powder

¼ tsp fine sea salt

2.5 oz (75 g) finely chopped hazelnuts, toasted

Rounded ½ cup (125 g) sour cream, at room temperature

3 tbsp (45 ml) whole milk, at room temperature

3 tbsp (45 ml) sunflower oil

Finely grated zest of 1 lemon

1 tsp vanilla extract

6 tbsp (¾ stick; 90 g) unsalted butter, at room temperature

⅔ cup (150 g) soft light brown sugar

2 large eggs, at room temperature

Cream Cheese Frosting
6 oz (175 g) white chocolate, at least 28%, finely chopped

8 oz (225 g) cream cheese, cold

4.5 oz (130 g) mascarpone cheese, cold

Finely grated zest of 2 lemons

Scant ½ cup (120 g) heavy cream, cold

Lemon slices and hazelnuts, for decorating (optional)

Make the cake: Preheat the oven to 350°F (175°C) or 325°F (160°C) if using a fan-assisted oven. Grease a 9-inch (23-cm) round springform pan with cooking spray or butter and line it with parchment paper.

Sift the flour, baking powder and salt into a medium-sized bowl. Add the toasted hazelnuts and whisk to combine. In a measuring jug, lightly whisk together the sour cream, milk, sunflower oil, lemon zest and vanilla.

In a large bowl, using an electric hand mixer, beat together the butter and brown sugar for 2 to 3 minutes on medium-high speed until the mixture turns pale and fluffy. Add the eggs, one at a time, making sure each is fully combined before adding the next. Scrape the bowl a couple of times with a silicone spatula to make sure everything is mixed nicely.

Next, add the flour mixture to the butter mixture in three additions, alternating with the sour cream mixture. After each addition beat the mixture just until everything is incorporated to avoid overmixing the cake.

Scrape the batter into the prepared pan and spread evenly. Bake for 40 to 45 minutes. The cake is done when it's springy on the top and when a skewer inserted into the middle comes out mostly clean. Once the cake is done, remove it from the oven, place it on a wire rack and let it cool in the pan for about 15 minutes before removing it from the pan to cool completely.

Make the frosting: Melt the white chocolate in a small, heatproof bowl set over a pan of simmering water. Alternatively, you can do this (using a microwave-safe bowl) in a microwave in 30-second intervals, stirring after each interval. Set aside to slightly cool.

In a large bowl, using an electric hand mixer, beat together the cream cheese, mascarpone cheese and lemon zest until creamy and combined. Add the melted chocolate and beat until fully incorporated.

In a separate bowl, beat the cream until soft peaks form. Carefully fold the whipped cream into the cream cheese mixture, until evenly combined.

Spread the frosting over the cooled cake and decorate with hazelnuts and twisted lemon slices, if desired.

Keep the cake tightly covered in plastic wrap or in an airtight container at room temperature for 2 days or in the fridge for up to a week. Allow it to come to room temperature before serving.

Carrot Walnut **Sheet Cake**

The humble carrot cake is one of the first cakes I learned to make, because I was genuinely intrigued with adding veggies to cake. Fast-forward a couple of years and it's everyone's favorite cake. Being basically a one-bowl cake, it's a great choice for beginners because it doesn't require any special techniques. In this recipe, the batter turns into the most delicious and moist, cinnamon-spiced carrot cake that manages to be both dense and fluffy at the same time—it sounds silly, but it's true! As it's topped with my all-time favorite orange cream cheese frosting, it will no doubt become your favorite, too.

Serves 12 to 14

Carrot Walnut Cake

6 oz (170 g) finely chopped walnuts

Cooking spray or butter, for pan

Scant 2½ cups (300 g) all-purpose flour

2½ tsp (12 g) baking powder

4 tsp (10 g) ground cinnamon

½ tsp fine sea salt

4 large eggs, at room temperature

½ tsp vanilla extract

Scant 1½ cups (320 g) soft light brown sugar

1 cup (240 ml) sunflower oil

11.5 oz (330 g) finely grated carrot (see Note)

Make the cake: In a dry skillet, briefly toast the walnuts over medium-high heat, until you smell the toasty aroma. This can take about 2 to 3 minutes. Remove from the heat and set aside to cool a little bit.

Preheat the oven to 350°F (175°C) or 325°F (160°C) if using a fan-assisted oven. Lightly grease with cooking spray or butter a 9 x 13-inch (23 x 33-cm) baking pan and line it with parchment paper that overhangs the two long sides for easier handling later.

Sift the flour, baking powder, cinnamon and salt into a large bowl. Add the toasted walnuts and whisk to combine. In the bowl of a stand mixer fitted with the whisk attachment, beat together the eggs, vanilla and brown sugar on medium-high speed until pale, fluffy and double in volume. Reduce the mixer speed to low and add the oil in a slow and steady stream. Beat until fully incorporated.

Next, add the flour mixture in two batches and beat until just incorporated. Scrape the bowl a couple of times with a silicone spatula to make sure everything is mixed nicely. Lastly, fold in the finely grated carrot.

Pour the batter into the prepared pan and spread evenly. Bake for 30 to 35 minutes. It's best to check the cake after 30 minutes and then adjust the baking time accordingly, because ovens can vary. The cake is done when it springs back if lightly touched and when a skewer inserted into the middle comes out mostly clean. Remove it from the oven and leave it to cool in the pans on a wire rack for 15 to 20 minutes to firm up a little bit before removing it from the pan to cool completely.

White Chocolate Cream Cheese Frosting

9 oz (250 g) white chocolate, at least 28%, finely chopped

12 oz (340 g) cream cheese, cold

7 oz (200 g) mascarpone cheese, cold

Finely grated zest of 1 orange

⅔ cup (160 g) heavy cream, cold

Chocolate shavings, candied orange peel and nuts, for decorating (optional)

Make the frosting: Place the white chocolate in a small, heatproof bowl and melt over a pan of simmering water. Alternatively, you can do this (using a microwave-safe bowl) in a microwave in 30-second intervals, stirring each time. Set aside to slightly cool.

In a large bowl, using an electric hand mixer, beat together the cream cheese, mascarpone cheese and orange zest, until creamy and combined. Add the melted chocolate and beat until fully incorporated. In a separate bowl, beat the cream until soft peaks form. Carefully fold the whipped cream into the cream cheese mixture, until evenly combined.

Spread the frosting over the cooled cake and decorate with chocolate shavings, orange peel and candied nuts, if desired.

Keep the cake tightly covered in plastic wrap or in an airtight container in the fridge for up to a week. Allow it to come to room temperature before serving.

Note: For the best sweet carrot flavor, use organic fresh carrots.

The Holidays

Ah, the holidays. That time of the year when everyone's inner baker comes out—and this year, I'm here to help you make the most of it! My favorite holiday has to be Christmas. Just hearing all the festive tunes puts me in baking mode. And the best part? All the happy faces and thumbs-ups afterward.

Between all the cookies, bars and other festive snacks, we make sure to have a cake as the centerpiece of our Christmas table. Something citrusy, such as Clementine Cranberry Layer Cake (page 171), is always at the top of the list. When you're feeling fancy, go for the Hazelnut Praline Yule Log (page 165), and if there's a Christmas Party (with a capital P), choose a boozy Banana Coconut Rum Bundt Cake (page 160).

To all those looking for a Thanksgiving showstopper, don't miss the Apple Crumble Custard Cake (page 153), which is basically a pie disguised in cake form, or the luscious Pumpkin Spice Chocolate Cake (page 151), which will have everyone asking for seconds.

Pumpkin Spice Chocolate Cake

I can't help it—I hop on the "pumpkin spice and everything nice" train the moment colder weather arrives, and especially so during the holidays. I mostly make my own pumpkin puree, because I don't have easy access to the canned one, but either one should work very well here. This warm, spiced pumpkin cake pairs incredibly with the light and silky chocolate frosting, making it the perfect introduction to the holiday season.

. . . .

Serves 12 to 14

Pumpkin Spice Cake
Cooking spray or butter, for pans

2 cups (250 g) all-purpose flour

2 tsp (10 g) baking powder

1½ tsp (3 g) ground cinnamon

¾ tsp ground ginger

½ tsp ground nutmeg

½ tsp ground cloves

¼ tsp ground cardamom

½ tsp fine sea salt

2 large eggs, at room temperature

¾ cup (150 g) granulated sugar

Rounded ½ cup (125 g) soft light brown sugar

½ cup (120 ml) sunflower oil

1 cup (250 g) pure pumpkin puree

½ tsp vanilla extract

Finely grated zest of 1 orange (optional)

Rounded ½ cup (120 g) sour cream, at room temperature

Chocolate Frosting
5.5 oz (150 g) 55% dark chocolate, finely chopped

1⅓ cups (2⅔ sticks; 300 g) unsalted butter, at room temperature

3½ tbsp (25 g) unsweetened cocoa powder

8.5 oz (240 g) condensed milk

¼ tsp fine sea salt

Make the cake: Preheat the oven to 350°F (175°C) or 325°F (160°C) if using a fan-assisted oven. Grease three 6-inch (15-cm) round cake pans with cooking spray or butter and line the bottoms with parchment paper.

Sift the flour, baking powder, cinnamon, ginger, nutmeg, cloves, cardamom and salt into a large bowl and whisk to combine. In a separate bowl, using an electric stand or hand mixer fitted with a whisk attachment, beat the eggs and the granulated and brown sugars on high speed until pale and doubled in volume, and the mixture falls like ribbons. While the mixer is running on low speed, pour in the oil in a slow and steady stream and beat until combined. Add the pumpkin puree, vanilla and orange zest (if using) and whisk to combine.

Switch to a paddle attachment and add the flour mixture in two batches, alternating with the sour cream. After each addition, mix the batter for about 15 seconds, or until everything is fully incorporated. Scrape the bowl a couple of times with a silicone spatula to make sure everything is getting mixed nicely.

Divide the batter equally by weight among the prepared pans and level it with an offset palette knife. Bake for 24 to 28 minutes. It's best to check the cakes after 24 minutes and then adjust the baking time accordingly, because ovens can vary. The cakes are done when they're springy on the top and when a skewer inserted into the middle comes out mostly clean. When they're done, remove them from the oven and leave them to cool in their pans on a wire rack for 10 to 15 minutes to firm up a little bit before removing them from the pans to cool completely.

Make the chocolate frosting: Melt the chocolate in a small, heatproof bowl set over a pot of simmering water. Make sure the bowl doesn't touch the water. Set aside to slightly cool.

Using a stand mixer fitted with the paddle attachment, beat the butter for 5 minutes, or until it's pale and fluffy. Sift in the cocoa powder and add the condensed milk along with the salt, and beat on medium-high speed until fully incorporated. Lastly, add the melted dark chocolate and beat until everything is evenly combined.

(continued)

Cinnamon sticks, star anise or other spices, for decorating (optional)

Assemble the cake: Start by leveling the tops of your cakes using a cake leveler or a long, serrated knife for a neater look, if needed. Put the buttercream into a large piping bag fitted with the open star nozzle. Then, put a little bit of frosting in the middle of a serving plate or your cake board to keep the cake from moving around. Place it on a turntable for easier handling and decorating.

Place 1 cake layer on the serving plate and pipe an even layer of frosting swirls across the entire top of the cake. Top with the next two layers, repeating the process for each (see Notes).

Decorate the top with cinnamon sticks and other whole spices, if desired.

Keep the cake tightly covered in plastic wrap or in an airtight container (see Notes) at room temperature for 2 days or in the fridge for up to a week. Allow it to come to room temperature before serving.

> **Notes:** If the frosting seems too soft, frost each layer individually, place in the fridge for 10 to 15 minutes to firm up and then stack the cake.
>
> Since the cake is left "naked," it can dry out quicker than other cakes if not stored and covered properly.

Apple Crumble *Custard* Cake

Crème mousseline is a French name for a frosting you may know as German buttercream or custard buttercream. It's made by combining vanilla pastry cream with beaten butter, and it produces a lovely, light vanilla buttercream. With brown butter cake layers, delicious apple pie filling that is sprinkled with nuggets of pie dough and a silky custard buttercream, this cake is nothing short of a delicious pie in disguise. If you want to switch things up on your Thanksgiving table, then this is the way to go.

. . . .

Serves 12 to 14

¾ cup + 2 tsp (1½ sticks + 2 tsp; 180 g) unsalted butter, sliced

Crème Mousseline
4 large egg yolks

1 large egg

⅓ cup (45 g) cornstarch

Rounded ¾ cup (160 g) granulated sugar

¼ tsp fine sea salt

2 cups + 2 tsp (490 ml) whole milk

2 tsp (10 ml) vanilla extract

1½ cups (3 sticks; 340 g) unsalted butter, at room temperature

Apple Pie Filling
2 Granny Smith apples

2 tbsp (30 g) unsalted butter

⅓ cup (75 g) soft light brown sugar

½ tsp ground cinnamon

¼ tsp fine sea salt

1 tbsp (8 g) cornstarch

½ cup (120 ml) water

Brown the butter: In a light-colored skillet, melt the sliced butter over medium-high heat, stirring constantly, until it becomes foamy, then turns clear and starts showing brown specks. You'll also notice a nutty aroma. Your butter is done after about 5 minutes, at a medium brown stage. Transfer the butter to a metal bowl and place in the fridge to firm up. Stir it occasionally so it firms up evenly and gets to a room-temperature consistency.

Begin the crème mousseline: In a medium-sized bowl, whisk together the egg yolks, egg, cornstarch, granulated sugar and salt. In a small, heavy-bottomed saucepan, bring the milk to a simmer over medium-high heat. Once the milk has reached the scalding point, about 5 minutes, turn off the heat and slowly pour about two-thirds of the milk into the egg mixture while whisking constantly so you don't cook the eggs. Once you have tempered the egg mixture, pour it back into the saucepan of the remaining milk and continue to cook, whisking constantly, until it thickens. After bubbles appear on the surface, continue to cook for another 1 to 2 minutes to get rid of the cornstarch flavor.

When the pastry cream is done cooking, stir in the vanilla and strain it through a sieve onto a big, shallow plate to get rid of any lumps and cooked egg bits. Cover with plastic wrap touching the surface to prevent a skin from forming, and let it cool to room temperature until needed.

Make the apple pie filling: Peel and core the apples and dice them into small cubes. In a small saucepan, combine the apple cubes with the butter, brown sugar, cinnamon and salt. Bring to a boil over medium heat, stirring gently with a spoon. In a small bowl, dilute the cornstarch with the water, and pour the mixture into the pan in a slow and steady stream, gently mixing constantly with a spoon until everything is incorporated.

Lower the heat and simmer for 4 to 5 minutes, or until the mixture thickens and the apples are tender but firm. Transfer the filling to a small bowl, cover with a piece of plastic wrap touching the surface and place it in the fridge to cool down.

(continued)

Apple Crumble *Custard* Cake (Continued)

Brown Butter Cake
Cooking spray or butter, for pans

2 cups (250 g) all-purpose flour

2 tsp (10 g) baking powder

½ tsp fine sea salt

¼ cup (60 ml) whole milk

Rounded ¾ cup (180 g) sour cream, at room temperature

3 tbsp (45 ml) sunflower oil

1 tsp vanilla extract

Reserved brown butter, at room temperature

Rounded cup (250 g) soft light brown sugar

3 large eggs, at room temperature

Pie Crumble
1 cup (125 g) all-purpose flour

3 tbsp (40 g) granulated sugar

Pinch of salt

⅓ cup (⅔ stick; 75 g) unsalted butter, melted

Make the cake: Preheat the oven to 350°F (175°C) or 325°F (160°C) if using a fan-assisted oven. Grease three 6-inch (15-cm) round cake pans with cooking spray or butter and line the bottoms with parchment paper.

Sift the flour, baking powder and salt into a medium-sized bowl and whisk to combine. In a measuring jug, lightly whisk together the whole milk, sour cream, sunflower oil and vanilla.

Using an electric stand or hand mixer, beat the room-temperature brown butter and brown sugar on medium-high speed for 2 to 3 minutes, or until the mixture turns pale and fluffy. Add the eggs, one at a time, making sure each is fully combined before adding the next. Scrape the bowl a couple of times with a silicone spatula to make sure everything is mixed nicely.

Next, add the flour mixture to the butter mixture in three additions, alternating with the sour cream mixture. After each addition, beat the mixture just until everything is incorporated to avoid overmixing the batter.

Divide the batter equally by weight among the prepared pans and level it with an offset palette knife. Bake for 22 to 25 minutes. It's best to check the cakes after 22 minutes and then adjust the baking time accordingly, because ovens can vary. The cakes are done when they're springy on the top and when a skewer inserted into the middle comes out mostly clean. When they're done, remove them from the oven and leave them to cool in their pans on a wire rack for 10 to 15 minutes to firm up a little bit before removing them from the pans to cool completely.

In the meantime, prepare the pie crumble: Preheat the oven to 400°F (205°C) or 375°F (190°C) if using a fan-assisted oven. Sift the flour, granulated sugar and salt into a small mixing bowl and combine with a fork. Add the melted butter and vigorously "cut" the mixture using a fork until it starts to look like little nuggets of dough. Spread the dough nuggets on a rimmed baking sheet lined with parchment paper, breaking them into smaller pieces if necessary. Bake for 15 to 20 minutes or until golden brown on the outside. Remove them from the oven and allow to cool completely before using.

Finish the crème mousseline: Using a stand mixer fitted with the paddle attachment, beat the butter for 5 minutes, or until it's pale and fluffy. Scrape the bowl a couple of times with a silicone spatula to ensure all the butter is being beaten, then add the previously made pastry cream, one spoonful at a time. Beat everything until it's all nicely incorporated with no lumps.

(continued)

Apple Crumble *Custard* Cake (Continued)

Apple chips, for decorating
(optional)

Assemble the cake: Start by leveling the tops of your cakes using a cake leveler or a long, serrated knife for a neater look, if needed. Then, put a little bit of buttercream in the middle of a serving plate or cake board to keep the cake from moving around. Place it on a turntable for easier handling and decorating.

Place one cake layer on the serving plate and, using a small, offset palette knife or a piping bag filled with buttercream, spread the frosting over the top of the cake layer, about ¼ inch (6 mm) thick. Make a dam around the edges, fill with the apple pie filling and scatter some pie crumb over them. Top it with the next cake layer and repeat the process. Place the final cake layer on top, making sure it's upside down to get a nice, smooth surface on top.

Next, apply a thin layer of frosting around the cake and smooth it using a cake scraper to keep in the crumbs. Chill the cake in the fridge for 30 to 60 minutes before applying the final coat of frosting and decorating. Once the crumb coat is firm, frost the cake with the remaining buttercream and make a swirl effect with an offset palette knife. Decorate the top with some buttercream dollops, leftover pie crumble and apple chips, if desired.

Keep the cake tightly covered in plastic wrap or in an airtight container at room temperature for 1 to 2 days or in the fridge for up to a week. Allow it to come to room temperature before serving.

Gingerbread *Latte* Sheet Cake

Inspired by the popular seasonal beverage, this cake hits all the right spots. Being a sheet cake, it's a ridiculously easy bake full of spicy, gingerbread flavor with light and silky frosting that brings out the coffee element. Topped with crunchy gingerbread cookies, it's in the run for the cutest (and tastiest!) holiday bake.

Serves 12 to 14

Latte Buttercream
Rounded ¼ cup (35 g) all-purpose flour

¾ cup (150 g) granulated sugar

¼ tsp fine sea salt

2½ tsp (5 g) ground instant espresso coffee

1⅛ cups (270 ml) whole milk

1⅛ cups (2¼ sticks; 250 g) unsalted butter, at room temperature

½ tsp vanilla extract

Gingerbread Cake
Cooking spray or butter, for pan

Rounded 2½ cups (320 g) all-purpose flour

2 tsp (3 g) ground cinnamon

1½ tsp (3 g) ground ginger

⅔ tsp ground nutmeg

⅓ tsp ground cloves

2½ tsp (12.5 g) baking powder

¼ tsp baking soda

¾ cup (150 g) granulated sugar

⅔ cup (150 g) soft light brown sugar

½ tsp fine sea salt

Rounded cup (240 g) sour cream, at room temperature

¼ cup (60 ml) sunflower oil

Rounded ¼ cup (100 g) dark molasses

3 large eggs, at room temperature

1 tsp vanilla extract

⅔ cup (1⅓ sticks; 150 g) unsalted butter, at room temperature

Zest of 1 orange

Begin the buttercream: In a small, heavy-bottomed saucepan, whisk together the flour, sugar, salt, instant coffee and milk. Cook over medium to high heat, whisking constantly so the mixture doesn't burn or catch on the bottom of the pan. Once it starts to thicken and you notice bubbling, cook for another 2 minutes, still whisking constantly, until it resembles pastry cream. This whole process could take up to 10 minutes.

When the pudding base is done, strain it through a sieve onto a shallow plate to get rid of any lumps. Cover it with plastic wrap touching the surface to prevent a skin from forming and let it cool to room temperature. You can speed up the process by letting it cool in the fridge, but prior to using, it must be room temperature.

Make the cake: Preheat the oven to 350°F (175°C) or 325°F (160°C) if using a fan-assisted oven. Lightly grease with cooking spray or butter a 9 x 13-inch (23 x 33–cm) baking pan and line it with parchment paper that overhangs the two long sides for easier handling later.

Sift the flour, cinnamon, ginger, nutmeg, cloves, baking powder, baking soda, granulated and brown sugars and salt into a bowl of a stand mixer, or a medium-sized bowl if you're using an electric hand mixer, and whisk to combine. In a measuring jug, lightly whisk together the sour cream, sunflower oil, molasses, eggs and vanilla. Add the butter to the flour mixture, fit the stand mixer with the paddle attachment and mix on low speed until you get a sandlike texture and there are no traces of flour.

Next, add the orange zest and the sour cream mixture in two equal batches to avoid splashing and overmixing the batter. After each addition, mix the batter for about 15 seconds, or until everything is fully incorporated. Scrape the bowl a couple of times with a silicone spatula to make sure everything is mixed nicely.

(continued)

Gingerbread *Latte* Sheet Cake (Continued)

Gingerbread cookies, for decorating (optional)

Scrape the batter into the prepared pan and level it using an offset palette knife, then bake for 35 to 40 minutes. It's best to check the cake after 30 minutes and then adjust the baking time accordingly, because ovens can vary. The cake is done when it's springy on the top and when a skewer inserted into the middle comes out mostly clean. Once it's done, remove from the oven and leave it to cool in the pan on a wire rack for 10 to 15 minutes to firm up a little bit before removing it from the pan to cool completely.

While the cake is cooling, finish the buttercream: Using a stand mixer fitted with the paddle attachment, beat the butter for 5 minutes, or until it's pale and fluffy, then add the previously made pudding base, one spoonful at a time. Beat everything until nicely incorporated with no lumps. Lastly, add the vanilla and beat for a couple of seconds, or until smooth and combined.

Once the cake is cool, cover it with frosting using an offset palette knife or a spoon, and decorate with gingerbread cookies (if using).

Keep the cake tightly covered in plastic wrap or in an airtight container at room temperature for 2 days or in the fridge for up to a week. Allow it to come to room temperature before serving.

Banana *Coconut Rum* Bundt Cake

This is one of my favorite bakes in this chapter, because it comes together really quickly and the combination of banana, coconut and my beloved rum makes it taste both a little tropical and festive. It's perfect when you want to make something special, but with no fuss in the kitchen.

. . . .

Serves 12 to 14

Cake
Cooking spray, for pan

2¼ cups (280 g) all-purpose flour

2½ tsp (12.5 g) baking powder

½ tsp ground cinnamon

1 cup (200 g) granulated sugar

Scant ½ cup (100 g) soft light brown sugar

½ tsp fine sea salt

Rounded cup (100 g) unsweetened desiccated coconut

1 cup + 2 tsp (250 g) coconut milk, at room temperature (see Note)

⅓ cup (80 ml) dark rum

3 large eggs, at room temperature

½ tsp vanilla extract

⅔ cup (1⅓ sticks; 150 g) unsalted butter, at room temperature

Scant ¼ cup (55 g) coconut oil, melted

Scant cup (200 g) overripe mashed banana (about 2 bananas)

Coconut Rum Glaze
1 tbsp (15 ml) dark rum

2 tbsp (30 ml) coconut milk

Rounded ¾ cup (100 g) powdered sugar

Coconut flakes, for decorating

Make the cake: Preheat the oven to 350°F (175°C) or 325°F (160°C) if using a fan-assisted oven. Spray a 10-cup (2.4 L) Bundt pan with cooking spray.

Sift the flour, baking powder, cinnamon, granulated and brown sugars and salt into the bowl of a stand mixer, or a medium-sized bowl if you're using an electric hand mixer. Add the desiccated coconut and whisk together.

In a measuring jug, lightly whisk together the coconut milk, rum, eggs and vanilla. Add the butter and coconut oil to the flour mixture, fit the stand mixer with the paddle attachment and mix on low speed until you get a sandlike texture and there are no traces of flour.

Next, add the mashed banana and the coconut milk mixture to the flour mixture in 3 equal batches to avoid splashing and overmixing the batter. After each addition, mix the batter for about 15 seconds, or until everything is fully incorporated. Scrape the bowl a couple of times with a silicone spatula to make sure everything is mixed nicely.

Scrape the batter into the prepared pan, level the top with an offset palette knife and bake for 45 to 50 minutes, or until a skewer inserted into the middle comes out mostly clean. It's best to check the cake after 40 minutes and then adjust the baking time accordingly, because ovens can vary. When the cake is done, remove it from the oven and allow it to cool in the pan for 15 minutes before carefully inverting it onto a wire rack to cool completely.

Make the coconut rum glaze: In a small bowl, whisk together the rum, coconut milk and powdered sugar. Add more sugar or liquid depending on the consistency you want. Pour the glaze over the cool cake, then sprinkle with coconut flakes before serving.

Store the cake in an airtight container at room temperature for 3 to 4 days or up to a week in the fridge.

> **Note:** Use the coconut milk that has at least 70 percent coconut, with water as the only additional ingredient. The best kind comes in a carton, but you can use some canned ones, too.

White Chocolate *Peppermint* Chocolate Cake

Chocolate and peppermint are a classic combination loved around the world and popular during the holidays. I admit, it took me some time to embrace it, but After Eight chocolates definitely helped me get there. This cake pairs rich and moist peppermint chocolate cake layers with creamy, peppermint white chocolate frosting, meaning double peppermint and double chocolate! Since peppermint is a very strong flavor, a little goes a long way, depending on the brand of extract you use—so err on the side of caution.

Serves 12 to 14

White Chocolate Buttercream

⅓ cup (40 g) all-purpose flour

Scant ⅔ cup (130 g) granulated sugar

¼ tsp fine sea salt

1½ cups (360 ml) whole milk

1⅓ cups (2⅔ sticks; 300 g) unsalted butter, at room temperature

1 tsp peppermint extract

7 oz (200 g) white chocolate, melted

Chocolate Cake

Cooking spray or butter, for pans

Scant 1½ cups (180 g) all-purpose flour

⅔ cup (75 g) Dutch-processed cocoa powder

2¼ tsp (12 g) baking powder

¾ cup (150 g) granulated sugar

⅔ cup (150 g) soft light brown sugar

½ tsp fine sea salt

Rounded ¾ cup (180 g) sour cream, at room temperature

½ cup (120 ml) sunflower oil

2 large eggs, at room temperature

1 tsp peppermint extract

½ cup + 1 tbsp (135 ml) hot water

Begin the buttercream: In a small, heavy-bottomed saucepan, whisk together the flour, sugar, salt and milk. Cook over medium to high heat, whisking constantly so the mixture doesn't burn or catch on the bottom of the pan. Once it starts to thicken and you notice bubbling, cook for another 2 minutes, still whisking constantly, until it resembles pastry cream. This whole process could take up to 10 minutes.

When the pudding base is done, strain it through a sieve onto a shallow plate to get rid of any lumps. Cover it with plastic wrap touching the surface to prevent a skin from forming and let it cool to room temperature. You can speed up the process by letting it cool in the fridge, but prior to using, it must be room temperature.

Make the cake: Preheat the oven to 350°F (175°C) or 325°F (160°C) if using a fan-assisted oven. Grease three 6-inch (15-cm) round cake pans with cooking spray or butter and line the bottoms with parchment paper.

Sift the flour, cocoa powder, baking powder, granulated and brown sugars and salt into a large bowl and whisk to combine. In a measuring jug, lightly whisk together the sour cream, sunflower oil, eggs and peppermint extract. Add the sour cream mixture to the flour mixture and whisk to combine into a thick batter. Lastly, add the hot water in 2 additions, whisking after each addition until smooth.

Divide the batter equally by weight among the prepared pans and level it with an offset palette knife. Bake for 23 to 28 minutes. It's best to check the cakes after 23 minutes and then adjust the baking time accordingly, because ovens can vary. The cakes are done if they spring back when lightly touched and when a skewer inserted into the middle comes out mostly clean. Remove them from the oven and leave them to cool in the pans for 10 minutes to firm up before transferring onto a wire rack to cool completely.

Finish the buttercream: Using a stand mixer fitted with the paddle attachment, beat the butter for 5 minutes, or until it's pale and fluffy, then add the previously made pudding base, one spoonful at a time. Beat everything until nicely incorporated with no lumps. Lastly, add the peppermint extract and melted white chocolate and beat until smooth and combined.

(continued)

White Chocolate *Peppermint* Chocolate Cake
(Continued)

Crushed candy canes, for decorating (optional)

Assemble the cake: Start by leveling the tops of your cakes, using a cake leveler or a long, serrated knife for a neater look, if needed. Then, put a little bit of buttercream in the middle of a serving plate or your cake board to keep the cake from moving around. Place it on a turntable for easier handling and decorating.

Place one cake layer on the serving plate and, using a small, offset palette knife or a piping bag filled with buttercream, spread the frosting over the top of the cake layer, about ⅜ inch (1 cm) thick. Top it with the next cake layer and repeat the process. Place the final cake layer on top, making sure it's upside down to get a nice, smooth surface on top.

Next, apply a thin layer of frosting around the cake and smooth it using a cake scraper to keep in the crumbs. Chill the cake in the fridge for 30 to 60 minutes before applying the final coat of frosting and decorating.

Once the crumb coat is firm you can frost the cake with the remaining buttercream or you can leave it naked and pipe French star nozzle buttercream dollops across the top of the cake. Decorate with crushed candy canes (if using).

Keep the cake tightly covered in plastic wrap or in an airtight container at room temperature for 2 days or in the fridge for up to a week. Allow it to come to room temperature before serving.

Note: This recipe makes enough buttercream to fully frost and decorate the whole cake; I just chose to do a naked version this time.

Hazelnut **Praline Yule Log**

Growing up, we never actually had a *bûche de Noël* for Christmas, but I would always admire it when going through various cookbooks. While the traditional French version includes a vanilla genoise sponge and chocolate buttercream filling, I wanted to make mine more luxurious for the holidays—and what a better way to do it than to include some hazelnuts? To still keep it French in its essence, I chose a luscious French buttercream flavored with hazelnut praline as a filling to a light, chocolate sponge.

. . . .

Serves 10 to 12

Hazelnut Praline

4.5 oz (125 g) blanched hazelnuts

Scant ⅔ cup (125 g) granulated sugar

2 tbsp + 1 tsp (35 ml) water

Pinch of fine sea salt

Chocolate Ganache

5.5 oz (150 g) 55% dark chocolate, finely chopped

½ cup + 1½ tbsp (150 g) heavy cream

Sponge Cake

Cooking spray or butter, for baking sheet

Rounded ½ cup (70 g) all-purpose flour

Rounded ¼ cup (30 g) unsweetened cocoa powder

½ tsp baking powder

¼ tsp fine sea salt

2 oz (50 g) ground hazelnuts, toasted

4 large eggs, at room temperature

¾ cup (150 g) granulated sugar

½ tsp vanilla extract

2 tbsp (30 ml) sunflower oil

Powdered sugar, for dusting kitchen towel

Make the hazelnut praline: First, in a dry skillet, toast the blanched hazelnuts over medium-high heat until golden brown and aromatic, about 3 minutes. Set aside until needed. Line a rectangular baking sheet with parchment paper.

In a small, heavy-bottomed saucepan, combine the granulated sugar and water and cook over medium-high heat until the sugar completely dissolves and reaches a golden amber color. Keep your eye on the saucepan at all times, because it can quickly go from beautifully caramelized to burned. Once it reaches the desired color, remove it from the heat, add the hazelnuts and stir very quickly. Then carefully dump the mixture onto the prepared tray and try to spread it as evenly as possible. Leave to set and cool, about 30 minutes.

After the caramel has set, break it into chunks and place in a food processor. Pulse for a couple of minutes, or until you get a smooth paste. Add the salt and store in a jar until needed.

Make the chocolate ganache: Place the dark chocolate in a medium-sized heatproof bowl. In a small saucepan, bring the cream to a simmer, then pour it over the chocolate. Cover with a plate and let sit 1 to 2 minutes, or until the chocolate starts to melt. Stir gently with a spatula until creamy, smooth and combined. Cover with plastic wrap touching the surface and leave at room temperature to set until spreadable.

Make the cake: Preheat the oven to 350°F (175°C) or 325°F (160°C) if using a fan-assisted oven. Grease a 10 x 15–inch (25 x 38–cm) baking sheet with cooking spray or butter and line it with parchment paper. Lightly grease the parchment paper, too.

Sift the flour, cocoa powder, baking powder and salt into a medium-sized bowl. Add the ground hazelnuts, whisk to combine and set aside. In a bowl of a stand mixer fitted with the whisk attachment, beat together the eggs, granulated sugar and vanilla on medium-high speed for 5 to 8 minutes, or until it becomes pale, doubles in size and falls off the beater in ribbons. Then, add the sunflower oil and mix until well incorporated. Lastly, gradually fold in the flour mixture until everything is combined.

(continued)

Filling

3 large egg yolks

1 large egg

Pinch of fine sea salt

½ cup (100 g) granulated sugar

¾ cup + 2 tsp (1½ sticks + 2 tsp; 180 g) unsalted butter, cubed, at room temperature

3.5 oz (100 g) hazelnut praline

2.5 oz (75 g) good-quality 55% dark chocolate, melted

½ tsp vanilla extract

Powdered sugar and meringue mushrooms (page 76), for decorating (optional)

Pour the batter onto the prepared baking sheet and spread evenly all the way into the corners using an offset palette knife. Bake for 12 to 15 minutes, or until the cake springs back to the touch. Check after 12 minutes and then adjust the baking time accordingly.

Generously sprinkle a clean kitchen towel with powdered sugar. This prevents the cake from sticking to the towel. When the cake is done baking, remove it from the oven and leave it in the pan for 2 minutes, then run a knife around the edges and flip the cake onto the towel. Carefully peel off the parchment paper and tightly roll up the cake within the towel. It's imperative to do this while it is still warm, otherwise it will crack later. Leave to cool.

Prepare the filling: In a large, heatproof bowl, vigorously whisk together the egg yolks, egg, salt and granulated sugar until combined. Place the bowl over a pan of simmering water, making sure it doesn't touch the water, and cook, whisking constantly, until the sugar dissolves.

Remove the bowl from the heat and beat with an electric hand or stand mixer on medium-high speed until the mixture is pale, doubles in volume and falls in ribbons. With the mixer still going on medium-low speed, add the butter, one cube at a time, and beat until fully incorporated. Lastly, add the hazelnut praline, melted chocolate and vanilla and beat until smooth and combined.

To assemble, unroll the cooled cake carefully and spread evenly with the filling using an offset palette knife. Carefully roll the cake back up and gently lift it onto a serving plate. Cover with chocolate ganache and make streaks, using an offset palette knife, to resemble a log.

Cut the ends thinly for a neater look, and if desired, decorate with meringue mushrooms and a light dusting of powdered sugar to resemble snow.

The cake is best the same day, but you can keep it in the fridge for a couple of days, tightly covered with plastic wrap to avoid drying. Allow it to come to room temperature before serving.

Maple Pecan Layer Cake

I really wanted to include candied nuts in one of the cakes in this book, and this cake seemed like the perfect choice. The candied pecans are made using a traditional method from my hometown, Dubrovnik—though it's usually used to make candied almonds—and they're one of my favorite things to snack on. To ensure a strong maple flavor in every bite, there's maple syrup both in the cake and in the beautiful, maple French buttercream. Toasted pecans in the cake provide a nice, toasty aroma, but the real stars here are the candied ones that make each bite taste like a sweet, crunchy heaven.

Serves 12 to 14

Candied Pecans
Scant ⅔ cup (125 g) granulated sugar

3 tbsp (45 ml) water

Pinch of salt

4.5 oz (125 g) pecans (see Notes)

Maple Buttercream
2 large eggs

3 large egg yolks

Rounded ⅓ cup (130 g) pure maple syrup (see Notes)

Pinch of fine sea salt

1½ cups (3 sticks; 340 g) unsalted butter, cubed, at room temperature

1 tsp vanilla extract

Maple Pecan Cake
Cooking spray or butter, for pans

2 cups (250 g) all-purpose flour

2 tsp (10 g) baking powder

¼ tsp baking soda

½ tsp fine sea salt

4.4 oz (120 g) finely chopped pecans, toasted

Rounded ¾ cup (180 g) sour cream, at room temperature

¾ cup (250 g) pure maple syrup

1 tsp vanilla extract

⅔ cup (1⅓ sticks; 150 g) unsalted butter, at room temperature

⅓ cup + 2 tbsp (100 g) soft light brown sugar

3 large eggs, at room temperature

Make the candied pecans: In a small, heavy-bottomed saucepan, bring the sugar, water and salt to a boil over high heat. Add the pecans and keep cooking on medium-high heat, stirring constantly, until the water evaporates and the sugar starts to crystallize and fully coats the nuts. This can take about 15 minutes. Once it's done and the nuts look dry and coated in sugar crystals, dump them onto a baking sheet lined with parchment paper, spread all over and leave to cool.

Make the buttercream: In a large heatproof bowl, vigorously whisk the eggs, egg yolks, maple syrup and salt until combined. Place the bowl over a pan of simmering water, making sure it doesn't touch the water, and cook, whisking constantly, until it thickens a little bit and reaches 145°F (64°C). Remove the bowl from the heat and beat with an electric hand or stand mixer on medium-high speed until the mixture is pale, doubles in volume and falls in ribbons. With the mixer still going on medium-low speed, add the butter, one cube at a time, and beat until fully incorporated. Add the vanilla and beat until combined.

Make the cake: Preheat the oven to 350°F (175°C) or 325°F (160°C) if using a fan-assisted oven. Grease three 6-inch (15-cm) round cake pans with cooking spray or butter and line the bottoms with parchment paper.

Sift the flour, baking powder, baking soda and salt into the bowl of a stand mixer, or a medium-sized bowl if you're using an electric hand mixer. Add the toasted pecans and whisk together. In a measuring jug, lightly whisk together the sour cream, maple syrup and vanilla. Using a stand mixer fitted with the paddle attachment, or a large bowl with an electric hand mixer, beat the butter with the brown sugar until pale and fluffy, 2 to 3 minutes. Add the eggs, one at a time, making sure each is fully incorporated before adding the next.

(continued)

Next, add the flour mixture to the butter mixture in three additions, alternating with the sour cream mixture to avoid splashing and overmixing the batter. After each addition, mix the batter just until combined. Scrape the bowl a couple of times with a silicone spatula to make sure everything is mixed nicely.

Divide the batter equally by weight among the prepared pans and level it with an offset palette knife. Bake for 22 to 25 minutes. It's best to check the cakes after 22 minutes and then adjust the baking time accordingly, because ovens can vary. The cakes are done when they're springy on the top and when a skewer inserted into the middle comes out mostly clean. Remove them from the oven and leave them to cool in their pans on a wire rack for 10 to 15 minutes to firm up a little bit before inverting them from the pans to a wire rack to cool completely.

Assemble the cake: Start by leveling the tops of your cakes using a cake leveler or a long, serrated knife for a neater look, if needed. Then, put a little bit of buttercream in the middle of a serving plate or cake board to keep the cake from moving around. Place it on a turntable for easier handling and decorating.

Place one cake layer on the serving plate and, using a small, offset palette knife or a piping bag filled with buttercream, spread the frosting over the top of the cake layer, about ⅜ inch (1 cm) thick, and sprinkle with candied pecans. Top it with the next cake layer and repeat the process. Place the final cake layer on top, making sure it's upside down to get a nice, smooth surface on top.

Next, apply a thin layer of frosting around the cake and smooth it using a cake scraper to keep in the crumbs. Chill the cake in the fridge for 30 to 60 minutes before applying the final coat of frosting and decorating. Once the crumb coat is firm, frost the cake with the remaining buttercream, smooth it using a cake scraper and make a swirl effect using an offset palette knife. Sprinkle the top with the candied pecans.

Keep the cake in an airtight container in the fridge for up to a week, but let it come to room temperature before serving.

Notes: You can use this method to make other candied nuts, as well.

Make sure to use a maple syrup with strong flavor; milder versions will lack in flavor.

Clementine Cranberry **Layer Cake**

I feel like this is such a classic flavor combination when December arrives, and I always look forward to it each year. The sweet and creamy white chocolate cream cheese frosting pairs perfectly with the tangy cranberry filling, while the clementine cake layers are so flavorful and tender that you'll want to eat them all on their own. If you find yourself without clementines, don't worry—you can use oranges instead, and it will still be very delicious.

. . . .

Serves 12 to 14

Cranberry Filling

Rounded ⅓ cup (200 g) frozen cranberries (see Note)

¼ cup (60 g) fresh clementine juice

Rounded ⅓ cup (80 g) granulated sugar

1 tbsp (8 g) cornstarch + 1 tbsp (15 ml) water

Clementine Cake

Cooking spray or butter, for pans

2 cups (250 g) all-purpose flour

2 tsp (10 g) baking powder

½ tsp fine sea salt

Rounded ⅔ cup (160 g) sour cream

3 tbsp (45 ml) sunflower oil

¼ cup + 1 tsp (75 g) fresh clementine juice

½ cup (1 stick; 115 g) unsalted butter

Finely grated zest of 2 clementines

1¼ cups (250 g) granulated sugar

3 large eggs

Make the cranberry filling: In a small, heavy-bottomed saucepan, bring the frozen cranberries, clementine juice and sugar to a boil over medium heat. Simmer for a few minutes, or until the cranberries release their juices. In a small bowl, dilute the cornstarch with the water, and pour the mixture over the cranberries in a slow and steady stream, mixing constantly with a large wooden spoon until everything is incorporated.

Bring the mixture back to a boil and cook for a few minutes until it becomes gloopy and thickens. If the filling is too thick, you can always add some more water, a splash at a time. Once thickened, transfer the filling to a bowl and cover with plastic wrap touching the surface to prevent a skin from forming. Leave at room temperature or in the fridge to cool completely.

Make the cake: Preheat the oven to 350°F (175°C) or 325°F (160°C) if using a fan-assisted oven. Grease three 6-inch (15-cm) round cake pans with cooking spray or butter and line the bottoms with parchment paper.

Sift the flour, baking powder and salt into a medium-sized bowl and whisk to combine. In a measuring jug, lightly whisk together the sour cream, sunflower oil and clementine juice.

Using a stand mixer fitted with the paddle attachment, beat the butter and clementine zest with half of the sugar until pale and fluffy, 2 to 3 minutes. Add the rest of the sugar and beat to combine. Add the eggs, one at a time, making sure each is fully incorporated before adding the next.

Next, add the flour mixture in three additions, alternating with the sour cream mixture to avoid splashing and overmixing the batter. After each addition, mix the batter just until combined. Scrape the bowl a couple of times with a silicone spatula to make sure everything is mixed nicely.

(continued)

Cream Cheese Frosting

9 oz (250 g) white chocolate, at least 28%, finely chopped

12 oz (340 g) cream cheese, cold

7 oz (200 g) mascarpone cheese, cold

Finely grated zest of 2 clementines

⅔ cup (160 g) heavy cream

Clementine twists or candied cranberries, for decorating (optional)

Note: I've never had the opportunity to see fresh cranberries, but feel free to use them instead of frozen ones. But since the frozen fruits release some extra liquid, you may want to add a splash of water to the pan to help with dissolving the sugar and cooking the fresh fruit.

Divide the batter equally by weight among the prepared pans and level it with an offset palette knife, then bake for 22 to 25 minutes. It's best to check the cakes after 22 minutes and then adjust the baking time accordingly, because ovens can vary. The cakes are done when they're springy on the top and when a skewer inserted into the middle comes out mostly clean. When they're done, remove them from the oven and leave them to cool in their pans on a wire rack for 10 to 15 minutes to firm up a little bit before removing them from the pans to cool completely.

Make the frosting: Place the white chocolate in a small, heatproof bowl and melt over a pan of simmering water. Alternatively, you can do this (using a microwave-safe bowl) in a microwave in 30-second intervals, stirring each time. Set aside to slightly cool.

In a large bowl, using an electric hand mixer, beat together the cold cream cheese and mascarpone cheese with the clementine zest until creamy and combined. Add the melted chocolate and beat until fully incorporated.

In a separate bowl, beat the cream until soft peaks form. Carefully fold the whipped cream into the cream cheese mixture, until evenly combined.

Assemble the cake: Start by leveling the tops of your cakes using a cake leveler or a long, serrated knife for a neater look, if needed. Then, put a little bit of frosting in the middle of a serving plate or your cake board to keep the cake from moving around. Place it on a turntable for easier handling and decorating.

Place one cake layer on the serving plate and, using a small, offset palette knife or a piping bag filled with buttercream, spread the frosting over the top of the cake layer, about ¼ inch (6 mm) thick. Make a dam around it and fill with cranberries. Top it with the next cake layer and repeat the process. Place the final cake layer on top, making sure it's upside down to get a nice, smooth surface on top.

Next, apply a thin layer of frosting around the cake and smooth it using a cake scraper to keep in the crumbs. Chill the cake in the fridge for 30 to 60 minutes before applying the final coat of frosting and decorating.

Once the crumb coat is firm, frost the cake with the remaining frosting and decorate with some clementine twists (if using) or candied cranberries (if using).

Keep the cake tightly covered in plastic wrap or in an airtight container at room temperature for 2 days or in the fridge for up to a week. Allow it to come to room temperature before serving.

Pistachio **White Chocolate Cheesecake**

This idea actually came from my pistachio macaron recipe. The glorious pistachio white chocolate ganache is one of our all-time favorite flavors, so I wanted to incorporate it into something less complicated than macarons. *Et voilà*, this amazing cheesecake was born! It's very creamy, it's full of rich pistachio flavor and it will have everyone asking for seconds—no doubt about it. There is also no water bath involved in this recipe, making the whole process a lot easier.

. . . .

Serves 10 to 12

Crust
Cooking spray or butter, for pan

9 oz (250 g) graham crackers or digestive biscuits

1 tbsp (15 g) soft light brown sugar

¼ tsp ground cinnamon

½ cup + 2 tsp (1 stick + 2 tsp; 125 g) unsalted butter, melted

Cheesecake Filling
5 oz (150 g) white chocolate, at least 28%, finely chopped

¾ cup + 1 tbsp (200 g) heavy cream

24 oz (680 g) full-fat cream cheese, at room temperature

⅔ cup (150 g) soft light brown sugar

Finely grated zest of ½ lemon

½ tsp ground cardamom

1 tsp vanilla extract

10.5 oz (300 g) pistachio paste (page 55)

3 large eggs, at room temperature

White Chocolate Ganache
4.5 oz (125 g) white chocolate, at least 28%, finely chopped

Scant ⅓ cup (75 g) heavy cream

White gel food coloring

Pistachios, for decorating

Make the crust: Preheat the oven to 350°F (175°C) or 325°F (160°C) if using a fan-assisted oven. Lightly grease with cooking spray or butter a 9-inch (23-cm) round springform pan and line the base with parchment paper.

In a food processor, pulse the graham crackers until finely ground. Add the brown sugar, cinnamon and melted butter and pulse until evenly combined. Transfer the mixture to the prepared pan and press firmly to create an even layer, pressing a little up the sides as well. Bake for 10 minutes, then remove it from the oven and set aside.

Make the filling: In a small, heatproof bowl, combine the white chocolate and cream and melt over a pan of simmering water. Stir to combine and set aside to cool while still remaining melted.

In a large bowl, using an electric hand mixer, beat the cream cheese, brown sugar, lemon zest, cardamom and vanilla until smooth and combined. Add the melted chocolate and pistachio paste, and beat until thoroughly combined. Add the eggs, one at a time, making sure each is fully incorporated before adding the next. Scrape the bowl a couple of times with a silicone spatula to make sure everything is getting mixed nicely. Pour the filling over the crust and spread into an even layer.

Bake for 35 to 40 minutes (see Note on page 48), or until the cheesecake is set around the edges, with a little wobble in the middle. Remove from the oven and leave it in the pan on a wire rack to cool to room temperature before putting in the fridge to cool completely, at least 4 hours.

Make the white chocolate ganache: Place the chocolate in a small, heatproof bowl. In a small saucepan, bring the cream to a simmer, then pour it over the chocolate. Cover with a plate and let sit for 1 to 2 minutes before stirring it to combine into a smooth and creamy chocolate ganache. Add some white gel food coloring and stir to combine. Leave aside to thicken a little bit.

When you're ready to serve, run a thin knife along the edges of the cheesecake and transfer it from the pan to a serving plate. Pour the white chocolate ganache on top and sprinkle with chopped pistachios around the edges.

Keep it covered in the fridge for 3 to 4 days.

Walnut **Mocha Cake**

There's an old, unwritten rule from decades ago, and it goes something like this: If your Christmas desserts don't have (wal)nuts in them, they're not really good and rich and are basically unworthy of your guests. The thinking was that, because nuts are fairly expensive, you needed to splurge to show off. That's why both of my grandmas would always have tons of walnut-based desserts, when I (not so) secretly really just wanted a lemon yogurt pie bar. So, to keep the tradition alive, I had to make a walnut cake for this book, and I paired it with the most decadent, coffee-flavored ganache—one that I've absolutely fallen in love with. The subtle coffee flavor also comes through in the soft and moist cake layers, making this an incredibly rich and delicious cake for any celebration.

Serves 12 to 14

Mocha Ganache Frosting
11 oz (300 g) dark chocolate, at least 55%, finely chopped

⅓ cup (300 g) heavy cream

¼ cup + 1 tsp (½ stick + 1 tsp; 60 g) unsalted butter

Pinch of salt

1 tbsp (6 g) ground instant espresso coffee (I prefer Nescafé brand)

Walnut Cake
Cooking spray or butter, for pans

2 cups (250 g) all-purpose flour

2 tsp (10 g) baking powder

½ tsp fine sea salt

4 oz (120 g) finely chopped walnuts, toasted

¼ cup (60 ml) whole milk, at room temperature

Rounded ⅔ cup (160 g) sour cream, at room temperature

1 tsp ground instant espresso coffee

1 tsp vanilla extract

⅔ cup (1⅓ sticks; 150 g) unsalted butter, at room temperature

Rounded cup (250 g) soft light brown sugar

3 large eggs, at room temperature

Make the frosting: Place the dark chocolate in a medium-sized, heatproof bowl. In a small saucepan, bring the cream, butter, salt and instant coffee to a simmer. Pour the mixture over the chocolate, cover with a plate and let it sit for 1 to 2 minutes, or until the chocolate starts to melt. Stir gently with a spatula until creamy, smooth and combined. Cover with plastic wrap touching the surface and leave at room temperature to set until spreadable.

Make the cake: Preheat the oven to 350°F (175°C) or 325°F (160°C) if using a fan-assisted oven. Grease three 6-inch (15-cm) round cake pans with cooking spray or butter and line the bottoms with parchment paper.

Sift and combine the flour, baking powder and salt in the bowl of a stand mixer, or a medium-sized bowl if you're using an electric hand mixer. Add the toasted walnuts and whisk together. In a measuring jug, lightly whisk together the milk, sour cream, instant coffee and vanilla.

Using a stand mixer fitted with the paddle attachment, or a large bowl and an electric hand mixer, beat the butter with half of the sugar until pale and fluffy, 2 to 3 minutes. Add the rest of the sugar and beat to combine. Add the eggs, one at a time, making sure each is fully incorporated before adding the next.

Next, add the flour mixture to the butter mixture in three additions, alternating with the sour cream mixture to avoid splashing and overmixing the batter. After each addition, mix the batter just until combined. Scrape the bowl a couple of times with a silicone spatula to make sure everything is mixed nicely.

Divide the batter equally by weight among the prepared pans and level it with an offset palette knife. Bake for 22 to 25 minutes. It's best to check the cakes after 22 minutes and then adjust the baking time accordingly, because ovens can vary. The cakes are done when they're springy on the top and when a skewer inserted into the middle comes out mostly clean. Remove them from the oven and leave them to cool in their pans on a wire rack for 10 to 15 minutes to firm up a little bit before inverting them from the pans onto a wire rack to cool completely.

Assemble the cake: Start by leveling the tops of your cakes using a cake leveler or a long, serrated knife for a neater look, if needed. Then, put a little bit of ganache in the middle of a serving plate or your cake board to keep the cake from moving around. Place it on a turntable for easier handling and decorating.

Place one cake layer on the serving plate and, using a small, offset palette knife or a piping bag filled with ganache, spread the frosting over the top of the cake layer, about ⅜ inch (1 cm) thick. Top it with the next cake layer and repeat the process. Place the final cake layer on top, making sure it's upside down to get a nice, smooth surface on top.

Next, apply a thin layer of frosting around the cake and smooth it using a cake scraper to keep in the crumbs. Chill the cake in the fridge for 30 to 60 minutes before applying the final coat of frosting.

Once the crumb coat is firm, frost the cake with the remaining ganache in a rustic manner.

Keep the cake tightly covered in plastic wrap or in an airtight container at room temperature for 2 days or in the fridge for up to a week. Allow it to come to room temperature before serving.

Classic Elegance

While I absolutely love experimenting in the kitchen, learning new things and coming up with fun flavor combinations, it's always good to have a couple of classics up my sleeve. While I do have to admit that most of these recipes fall into the category of learning new things for me, I know that for most Americans they will bring back fond memories or help create new ones.

When I was starting my layer cake baking journey, Red Velvet Cake (page 200) was obviously the most intriguing because of its color, and let me tell you— its recognizable looks and mildly sweet flavor won me (and everyone else I know!) over.

I can never say no to a classic Marble Bundt Cake (page 181), which my mum would often make as a quick sheet cake on the weekends when nothing sweet was around. I loved eating it just slightly warm from the pan, and I'm sure you will, too.

Anything with a custard filling, such as a simple Boston Cream Pie (page 189) is always the top choice for the men in my family, and if you're looking for celebratory cakes, look no further—my versions of Chocolate Yellow Birthday Cake (page 182) and Funfetti Sheet Cake (page 195) are here to make birthdays extra delicious, but also easier on the brave parents hosting children's parties.

So, dive into these classic (and classically delicious!) recipes, and enjoy the old, new and tasty memories to your heart's content!

Marble **Bundt Cake**

This cake is pure comfort. A classic I'm sure many of us grew up with, no matter the shape in which it was baked. Chocolate and vanilla—the best of both worlds—come together here in one simple, delicious and beautiful-looking cake. Enjoy!

. . . .

Serves 12 to 14

Cake
Cooking spray, for pan

Rounded ¼ cup (30 g)
Dutch-processed cocoa powder

3 to 4 tbsp (45 to 60 ml) hot water

Rounded 2¾ cups (350 g)
all-purpose flour

1 tbsp (14 g) baking powder

¾ tsp fine sea salt

Rounded cup (240 g) sour cream,
at room temperature

⅓ cup (80 ml) whole milk, at room
temperature

¼ cup (60 ml) sunflower oil

2 tsp (10 ml) vanilla extract

¾ cup (1½ sticks; 170 g) unsalted
butter, at room temperature

1¾ cups (350 g) granulated sugar

4 large eggs, at room
temperature

Chocolate Glaze
3.5 oz (100 g) 55% dark chocolate,
finely chopped

½ cup (125 g) heavy cream

Make the cake: Preheat the oven to 350°F (175°C) or 325°F (160°C) if using a fan-assisted oven. Grease a 10-cup (2.4 L) or 12-cup (2.9 L) Bundt pan with cooking spray.

In a small bowl, whisk together the cocoa powder and hot water to form a paste. Set aside until needed. Sift the flour, baking powder and salt into a large bowl and whisk to combine. In a measuring jug, lightly whisk together the sour cream, milk, sunflower oil and vanilla.

Using a stand mixer fitted with the paddle attachment, or a large bowl and an electric hand mixer, beat the butter with half of the sugar until pale and fluffy, 2 to 3 minutes. Add the rest of the sugar and beat to combine. Add the eggs, one at a time, making sure each is fully incorporated before adding the next.

Next, add the flour mixture to the butter mixture in three additions, alternating with the sour cream mixture to avoid splashing and overmixing the batter. After each addition, mix the batter just until combined. Scrape the bowl a couple of times with a silicone spatula to make sure everything is mixed nicely.

Transfer about one-third of the batter to a separate, medium-sized bowl. Add a couple of tablespoons (about 30 ml) of that batter to the cocoa powder paste, stir until thoroughly combined, return it to the bowl of batter it came from, then fold to create the chocolate part.

Pour half of the vanilla batter from the large bowl into the prepared pan, top it with the chocolate batter and finish with the second half of the vanilla batter. Using a palette knife or a skewer, make swirls in a figure-8 motion. Do this two to four times, no more, otherwise you might lose the marble effect.

Bake for 50 to 55 minutes, or until a skewer inserted into the middle comes out mostly clean. It's best to check the cake after 45 minutes and then adjust the baking time accordingly, because ovens can vary. When the cake is done, remove it from the oven and allow to cool in the pan for 15 minutes before carefully inverting it onto a wire rack to cool completely.

Make the chocolate glaze: Place the chocolate in a small, heatproof bowl. In a small saucepan, bring the cream to a simmer, then pour it over the chocolate. Cover with a plate and let it sit for 1 to 2 minutes, then stir with a spatula until combined and smooth. Once the cake is cooled, transfer it to a serving plate and pour the chocolate glaze over it.

Chocolate Yellow **Birthday Cake**

The most beloved and popular birthday cake flavor of all time deserves its place in the Classics section. To make the yellow in this yellow cake stand out just a little bit more, I added two egg yolks to my batter, which also makes the cake that much more tender. This extremely easy chocolate frosting whips up in no time to give you an exceptionally milky, chocolate frosting that both kids and adults will adore. Throw in some sprinkles and you're good to go!

. . . .

Serves 12 to 14

Yellow Cake

Cooking spray or butter, for pans

2 cups (250 g) all-purpose flour

2 tsp (10 g) baking powder

½ tsp fine sea salt

Rounded ¾ cup (180 g) sour cream, at room temperature

¼ cup (60 ml) whole milk, at room temperature

1 tbsp (15 ml) vanilla extract

⅔ cup (1⅓ sticks; 150 g) unsalted butter, at room temperature

1¼ cups (250 g) granulated sugar

2 large eggs, at room temperature

2 large egg yolks, at room temperature (see Note)

Make the cake: Preheat the oven to 350°F (175°C) or 325°F (160°C) if using a fan-assisted oven. Grease three 6-inch (15-cm) round cake pans with cooking spray or butter and line the bottoms with parchment paper.

Sift the flour, baking powder and salt into a medium-sized bowl and whisk to combine. In a measuring jug, lightly whisk together the sour cream, milk and vanilla.

Using a stand mixer fitted with the paddle attachment, or a large bowl and an electric hand mixer, beat the butter with half of the sugar until pale and fluffy, 2 to 3 minutes. Add the rest of the sugar and beat to combine. Add the eggs and egg yolks, one at a time, making sure each is fully incorporated before adding the next.

Next, add the flour mixture to the butter mixture in three additions, alternating with the sour cream mixture to avoid splashing and overmixing the batter. After each addition, mix the batter just until combined. Scrape the bowl a couple of times with a silicone spatula to make sure everything is mixed nicely.

Divide the batter equally by weight among the prepared pans and level it with an offset palette knife. Bake for 22 to 25 minutes. It's best to check the cakes after 22 minutes and then adjust the baking time accordingly, because ovens can vary. The cakes are done when they're springy on the top and when a skewer inserted into the middle comes out mostly clean. Remove them from the oven and leave them to cool in their pans on a wire rack for 10 minutes to firm up a little bit before inverting them from the pans onto a wire rack to cool completely.

(continued)

Chocolate Frosting

5.5 oz (150 g) 55% dark chocolate, finely chopped

1⅓ cups (2⅔ sticks; 300 g) unsalted butter, at room temperature

Scant ¼ cup (25 g) unsweetened cocoa powder

8.5 oz (240 g) condensed milk

¼ tsp fine sea salt

Rainbow sprinkles, for decorating

Make the frosting: Melt the chocolate in a small, heatproof bowl set over a pot of simmering water. Make sure the bowl doesn't touch the water. Set aside to cool slightly.

Using a stand mixer fitted with the paddle attachment, beat the butter for 5 minutes, or until it's pale and fluffy. Sift in the cocoa powder and add the condensed milk along with the salt, and beat on medium-high speed until fully incorporated. Lastly, add the melted dark chocolate and beat until everything is evenly combined.

Assemble the cake: Start by leveling the tops of your cakes using a cake leveler or a long, serrated knife for a neater look, if needed. Then, put a little bit of frosting in the middle of a serving plate or cake board to keep the cake from moving around. Place it on a turntable for easier handling and decorating.

Place one cake layer on the serving plate and using a small, offset palette knife or a piping bag filled with frosting, spread the frosting over the top of the cake layer, about ⅜ inch (1 cm) thick. Place the final cake layer on top, making sure it's upside down to get a nice, smooth surface on top.

Next, apply a thin layer of frosting around the cake and smooth it using a cake scraper to keep in the crumbs. Chill the cake in the fridge for 30 to 60 minutes before applying the final coat of frosting and decorating.

Once the crumb coat is firm, frost the cake with the remaining frosting in a rustic manner and decorate with sprinkles, if desired.

Keep the cake tightly covered in plastic wrap or in an airtight container at room temperature for 2 days or in the fridge for up to a week. Allow it to come to room temperature before serving.

Note: You can freeze leftover egg whites for up to a year. Thaw them gradually in the fridge, then allow to come to room temperature before using.

Neapolitan **Layer Cake**

I wonder how many of us associate that delicious chocolate-vanilla-strawberry block of Neapolitan ice cream with our childhood. For me, it was one of the best things to eat, and I couldn't wait to cake-ify those flavors. But instead of going the usual route of doing everything in three, I decided to make a fun marble cake and pair it with silky and delicious strawberry frosting. Of course, I couldn't skip the signature look on the outside, which is easier to make than you think, trust me. Throw in some sprinkles, chocolate and wafers, and there you have it—the most incredible Neapolitan cake, which both kids and adults will adore!

. . . .

Serves 10 to 12

Marble Cake
Cooking spray or butter, for pans

Scant 2 tbsp (12 g) Dutch-processed cocoa powder

1 to 2 tbsp (15 to 30 ml) hot water

2 cups (250 g) all-purpose flour

2 tsp (10 g) baking powder

½ tsp fine sea salt

¼ cup (60 ml) whole milk, at room temperature

Rounded ¾ cup (180 g) sour cream, at room temperature

3 tbsp (45 ml) sunflower oil

2 tsp (10 ml) vanilla extract

½ cup (1 stick; 115 g) unsalted butter, at room temperature

Rounded 1¼ cups (260 g) granulated sugar

3 large eggs, at room temperature

Make the cake: Preheat the oven to 350°F (175°C) or 325°F (160°C) if using a fan-assisted oven. Grease three 6-inch (15-cm) round cake pans with cooking spray or butter and line the bottoms with parchment paper.

In a small bowl, whisk together the cocoa powder and hot water to form a paste. Set aside until needed. Sift the flour, baking powder and salt into a medium-sized bowl and whisk to combine. In a measuring jug, lightly whisk together the milk, sour cream, sunflower oil and vanilla.

Using a stand mixer fitted with the paddle attachment, beat the butter with half of the sugar until pale and fluffy, 2 to 3 minutes. Add the rest of the sugar and beat to combine. Add the eggs, one at a time, making sure each is fully incorporated before adding the next.

Next, add the flour mixture in three additions, alternating with the sour cream mixture to avoid splashing and overmixing the batter. After each addition, mix the batter just until combined. Scrape the bowl a couple of times with a silicone spatula to make sure everything is mixed nicely.

Weigh your batter and divide it equally between two bowls. Set one of the bowls aside to remain vanilla flavored. Transfer a couple of tablespoons (about 30 ml) of batter from the second bowl to a small bowl and whisk in the cocoa powder paste, then return that mixture to the bowl it came from and mix, using a spatula, until you get a smooth chocolate batter.

Divide the batter as equally as possible among three pans, spooning in a bit of vanilla batter and a little bit of chocolate batter alternately to create a marble effect in each pan. Once you're done spooning your batter, using a palette knife or a skewer, make swirls in a figure-8 motion. Do this two to four times, no more, otherwise you might lose the marble effect.

Bake the cakes for 20 to 25 minutes. It's best to check the cakes after 20 minutes and then adjust the baking time accordingly, because ovens can vary. The cakes are done when they're springy on the top and when a skewer inserted into the middle comes out mostly clean. When they're done, remove them from the oven and leave them to cool in their pans on a wire rack for 10 to 15 minutes to firm up a little bit before removing them from the pans to cool completely.

(continued)

Strawberry Jam

10.5 oz (300 g) fresh or frozen strawberries

3 tbsp (40 g) granulated sugar

1 tbsp (15 ml) water

Three-Color Buttercream

Scant ½ cup (55 g) all-purpose flour

Rounded cup (225 g) granulated sugar

½ tsp fine sea salt

Scant 1⅔ cups (390 ml) whole milk

1½ cups (3 sticks; 340 g) unsalted butter, at room temperature

2 tsp (10 ml) vanilla extract

3 to 4 tbsp (45 to 60 ml) thick strawberry jam

Red gel food coloring (optional)

2.5 oz (75 g) good-quality 60% dark chocolate, finely chopped

Make the strawberry jam: In a small saucepan, bring the strawberries, sugar and water to a simmer over medium-high heat, stirring occasionally so the mixture doesn't catch on the bottom of the pan. Press the strawberries with the back of the silicone spatula or a wooden spoon to speed up the process. Simmer until the mixture is thick, 15 to 20 minutes. Remove from the heat, strain through a sieve or puree it with an immersion blender, cover with plastic wrap touching the surface to prevent a skin from forming and let cool completely before using.

Begin the buttercream: In a small, heavy-bottomed saucepan, whisk together the flour, sugar, salt and milk. Cook over medium to high heat, whisking constantly so the mixture doesn't burn or catch on the bottom of the pan. Once it starts to thicken and you notice bubbling, cook for another 2 minutes, still whisking constantly, until it resembles pastry cream. This whole process could take up to 10 minutes.

When the pudding base is done, strain it through a sieve onto a shallow plate to get rid of any lumps. Cover it with plastic wrap touching the surface to prevent a skin from forming and let it cool to room temperature. You can speed up the process by letting it cool in the fridge, but prior to using, it must be room temperature.

Using a stand mixer fitted with the paddle attachment, beat the butter for 5 minutes, or until it's pale and fluffy, then add the previously made pudding base, one spoonful at a time. Beat everything until nicely incorporated with no lumps. Add the vanilla and mix until creamy and combined.

Now, make the frosting: Transfer half of the buttercream to a separate medium-size bowl. To that bowl, mix in the strawberry jam, and for a more intense color, add a little bit of red gel food coloring.

Transfer half of the remaining untinted buttercream to a smaller bowl. Place the dark chocolate in a small, heatproof bowl and melt over a pot of simmering water. Let it cool a little bit, then add it to one bowl of untinted buttercream and mix using a silicone spatula, until thoroughly combined. Leave the remaining buttercream that remains in its original bowl as is to use as vanilla frosting.

Assemble the cake: Start by leveling the tops of your cakes using a cake leveler or a long, serrated knife for a neater look, if necessary. Then, put a little bit of buttercream in the middle of a serving plate or cake board to keep the cake from moving around. Place it on a turntable for easier handling and decorating.

(continued)

Dark Chocolate Ganache

2 oz (60 g) good-quality dark chocolate, finely chopped

Scant ⅓ cup (70 g) heavy cream

Chocolate wafers and sprinkles, for decorating (optional)

Place one cake layer on a serving plate and, using a small, offset palette knife or a piping bag, spread or pipe the strawberry buttercream over the top of the cake layer, about ½ inch (1 cm) thick. Drizzle with some strawberry jam, then top it with the next cake layer and repeat the process, still using the strawberry frosting. Place the final cake layer on top, making sure it's upside down to get a nice, smooth surface on top. Next, apply a thin layer of the strawberry frosting around the cake and smooth it using a cake scraper. Chill the cake in the fridge for 30 to 60 minutes before decorating.

Visually divide the cake into three equal parts. Starting at the bottom third, apply the chocolate frosting using a small offset palette knife or a piping bag fitted with a round nozzle. Next, apply the white vanilla frosting on the middle third using the same technique. It's okay if they overlap a little bit. Lastly, cover the top third and the top of the cake with the remaining strawberry frosting. When you're done covering the cake with all three colors, smooth the sides of the cake by lightly pressing it with a cake scraper and occasionally wiping it with a paper towel for a neater look.

Chill the cake for half an hour to an hour before putting the chocolate drip on top.

Make the dark chocolate ganache: Place the chocolate in a small, heatproof bowl. In a small saucepan, bring the cream to a simmer, then pour it over the chocolate. Cover with a plate and let sit for 1 to 2 minutes, or until the chocolate softens and begins to melt. Stir with a spatula until combined and smooth. Alternatively, you can do this (using a microwave-safe bowl) in a microwave in 30-second intervals. If it seems too loose, leave it to cool and thicken for 10 to 15 minutes before pouring over the chilled cake.

When your cake is chilled and you're ready to decorate, pour two-thirds of the dark chocolate ganache onto the middle of your cake and slowly spread it around with a small offset palette knife for a natural-looking drip. If you need more, add the remaining third of the ganache on top and spread it in the same manner. You might end up with a little leftover ganache.

Put the cake in the fridge so the chocolate drip has time to set. Then, pipe any leftover buttercream across the middle top of the cake, and decorate with chocolate wafers and sprinkles.

Keep the cake tightly covered in plastic wrap or in an airtight container at room temperature for 2 days or in the fridge for up to a week. Allow it to come to room temperature before serving.

Boston Cream **Pie**

Ah, the age-old question: Is Boston cream pie a pie or a cake? It turns out it's a cake that was baked in a pie pan back in the 18th century—hence the name. The tender and tangy buttermilk vanilla cake layers are sandwiched together with a delicious, rich pastry cream to create a glorious ode to vanilla. Top it off with some chocolate ganache and you have a stunning-looking dessert in an instant. Another great thing about this recipe is that you now have a perfect pastry cream recipe that you can use as a filling to doughnuts, éclairs and more.

Serves 10 to 12

Vanilla Pastry Cream
4 large egg yolks

1 large egg

⅓ cup (45 g) cornstarch

Rounded ¾ cup (160 g) granulated sugar

¼ tsp fine sea salt

2 cups + 2 tsp (490 ml) whole milk

2 tsp (10 ml) vanilla extract

Buttermilk Vanilla Cake
Cooking spray or butter, for pans

2 cups (250 g) all-purpose flour

2 tsp (10 g) baking powder

½ tsp fine sea salt

¾ cup + 1 tbsp (200 g) buttermilk, at room temperature (see Note)

3 tbsp (45 ml) sunflower oil

2 tsp (10 ml) vanilla extract

⅔ cup (1⅓ sticks; 150 g) unsalted butter, at room temperature

1¼ cups (250 g) granulated sugar

3 large eggs, at room temperature

Make the pastry cream: In a medium-sized bowl, whisk together the egg yolks, egg, cornstarch, sugar and salt. In a small saucepan, bring the milk to a simmer over medium-high heat. Once the milk has reached the scalding point, turn off the heat and slowly pour around two-thirds of the milk into the egg mixture while whisking constantly so you don't cook the eggs. Once you have tempered the egg mixture, pour it back into the saucepan of the remaining milk and continue to cook, whisking constantly, until it thickens. After bubbles appear on the surface, which should take about 2 minutes, continue to cook for another 2 minutes to get rid of the cornstarch flavor.

When the pastry cream is done, stir in the vanilla and strain it through a sieve onto a big, shallow plate to get rid of any possible lumps and cooked egg bits. Cover with plastic wrap touching the surface to prevent a skin from forming, and let it cool to room temperature before putting in the fridge to cool completely.

Make the cake: Preheat the oven to 350°F (175°C) or 325°F (160°C) if using a fan-assisted oven. Grease two 8-inch (20 cm) round cake pans with cooking spray or butter and line the bottoms with parchment paper.

Sift the flour, baking powder and salt into a medium-sized bowl and whisk to combine. In a measuring jug, lightly whisk together the buttermilk, sunflower oil and vanilla.

Using a stand mixer fitted with the paddle attachment, beat the butter with half of the sugar until pale and fluffy, 2 to 3 minutes. Add the rest of the sugar and beat for another minute, or until combined. Add the eggs, one at a time, making sure each is fully incorporated before adding the next. Add the flour mixture to the butter mixture in 3 additions, alternating with the buttermilk mixture to avoid overmixing the batter. Scrape the bowl a couple of times with a silicone spatula to make sure everything is mixed nicely.

(continued)

Chocolate Ganache

4.5 oz (125 g) 55% dark chocolate, finely chopped

½ cup + 1½ tbsp (150 g) heavy cream

Divide the batter equally by weight among the prepared pans and level it with an offset palette knife, then bake for 20 to 25 minutes. It's best to check the cakes after 20 minutes and then adjust the baking time accordingly, because ovens can vary. The cakes are done when they're springy on the top and when a skewer inserted into the middle comes out mostly clean. When they're done, remove them from the oven and leave them to cool in their pans on a wire rack for 10 to 15 minutes to firm up a little bit before removing them from the pans to cool completely.

Assemble the cake: Whip the cold pastry cream using a stand mixer fitted with a whisk attachment, or an electric hand mixer, until creamy. Transfer it into a large piping bag fitted with a French open star nozzle. Level the tops of your cakes using a cake leveler or a long, serrated knife for a neater look, if needed.

Place one cake layer on a serving plate and pipe dollops of pastry cream all over to create an even layer. Carefully place the second cake layer on top, making sure it's upside down to get a nice smooth surface on top. Don't press it too much so the pastry cream doesn't ooze out. Gently place the cake in the fridge to chill for 15 minutes while you prepare the chocolate ganache.

Make the chocolate ganache: Place the chocolate in a small, heatproof bowl. In a small saucepan, bring the cream to a simmer, then pour it over the chocolate. Cover with a plate and let sit for 1 to 2 minutes before stirring it to combine into a smooth and creamy chocolate ganache.

Pour the ganache over the cake and spread using an offset palette knife.

Keep the cake covered in the fridge for up to 5 days. Allow it to come to room temperature before serving.

Note: If you don't have buttermilk, you can make a substitute by mixing ¾ cup plus 1½ tablespoons (200 ml) of whole milk with 2 tablespoons (30 ml) of fresh lemon juice. Leave it for 10 to 15 minutes, or until it thickens.

Lemon Poppy Seed Drizzle Cake

I think it's been pretty clear so far how much I love lemon and other citrus desserts, and this classic drizzle cake is no exception. The cake is already pretty moist and delicious on its own, but that drizzle is essential in making it a classic and providing even more zesty lemon flavor. Just think of this cake as the perfect everyday treat! I wanted to make it a tiny bit fancier, so I topped it with some candied lemon and orange peel, but you can most certainly leave that out because, if you're anything like me, you'll end up eating it more than using it for decorating. Oopsie.

. . . .

Serves 12 to 14

Lemon Poppy-Seed Cake

Cooking spray or butter, for pan

1¾ cups (220 g) all-purpose flour

2 tsp (10 g) baking powder

½ tsp fine sea salt

¼ cup (50 g) poppy seeds, plus more for decorating

Rounded ¾ cup (180 g) sour cream, at room temperature

3 tbsp (45 ml) sunflower oil

¼ cup (60 ml) fresh lemon juice

½ cup (1 stick; 115 g) unsalted butter, at room temperature

Zest of 2 lemons

Rounded cup (225 g) granulated sugar

3 large eggs, at room temperature

Make the cake: Preheat the oven to 350°F (175°C) or 325°F (160°C) if using a fan-assisted oven. Grease with cooking spray or butter and line with parchment paper a 9 x 5–inch (23 x 13–cm) loaf pan. If you have a smaller pan on hand, you'll end up with leftover batter, which you can bake as cupcakes.

Sift together the flour, baking powder and salt into a medium-sized bowl. Add the poppy seeds and whisk together. In a measuring jug, lightly whisk together the sour cream, sunflower oil and lemon juice.

In a large bowl, using an electric hand mixer, beat together the butter and lemon zest for 2 to 3 minutes on medium-high speed until the mixture turns pale and fluffy. Add the granulated sugar and beat until combined. Add the eggs, one at a time, making sure each is fully combined before adding the next. Scrape the bowl a couple of times with a silicone spatula to make sure everything is mixed nicely.

Next, add the flour mixture to the butter mixture in three additions, alternating with the sour cream mixture. After each addition, beat the mixture just until everything is incorporated to avoid overmixing the batter.

Fill the loaf pan about three-quarters of the way full with the cake batter. Using an offset palette knife, smooth out the top. Bake for 45 to 50 minutes. The cake is done when it's springy on the top and when a skewer inserted into the middle comes out mostly clean. Once the cake is done, remove it from the oven, place it on a wire rack and let it cool in the pan for about 15 minutes.

(continued)

Lemon Syrup
Rounded ⅓ cup (75 g) granulated sugar

Juice of 2 lemons (about 5 tbsp [75 ml])

Lemon Glaze
1 to 2 tbsp (15 to 30 ml) fresh lemon juice

1¼ cups (150 g) powdered sugar

Candied lemon and orange peel, for decorating

Meanwhile, prepare the lemon syrup: In a small, nonreactive saucepan, combine the sugar and lemon juice and cook over medium-high heat until the sugar dissolves and the mixture comes to a simmer. Turn off the heat and set aside.

Gently transfer the cake from the pan onto a wire rack set above a baking sheet lined with parchment paper. Poke the cake all over with a skewer or a toothpick and generously brush with lemon syrup. Leave to cool completely before pouring the glaze over the cake.

Make the lemon glaze: In a small, nonreactive bowl, simply whisk together the lemon juice and powdered sugar until you get your desired consistency. For a thicker glaze, add more sugar; for a thinner one, add more juice. Pour the glaze over the cake and decorate it with candied lemon peel and additional poppy seeds, if desired.

Keep the cake tightly covered in plastic wrap or in an airtight container at room temperature for 2 days or in the fridge for up to a week. Allow it to come to room temperature before serving.

 **Sheet Cake**

Every baker should have a great vanilla sheet cake recipe in their arsenal and that's exactly what I'm giving you here. It's tender, moist and absolutely delicious—packed full of vanilla both in the silky ermine buttercream and the cake. Since that's the only flavor in this cake, feel free to splurge on a good quality extract. If you're making this cake for a children's birthday party, instead of sprinkling the cake with extra rainbow sprinkles, choose some M&M's or European Smarties, if you can get your hands on them—the kids will love it (and the adults, too!).

Serves 16 to 18

Vanilla Buttercream
Rounded ¼ cup (35 g) all-purpose flour

⅔ cup (130 g) granulated sugar

¼ tsp fine sea salt

1⅛ cups (280 g) whole milk

1⅛ cups (2¼ sticks; 250 g) unsalted butter, at room temperature

2 tsp (10 ml) vanilla extract

Rose gel food coloring (optional)

Funfetti Vanilla Cake
Cooking spray or butter, for pan

Rounded 2½ cups + 1 tbsp (328 g) all-purpose flour, divided

2½ tsp (12.5 g) baking powder

½ tsp fine sea salt

⅓ cup (80 ml) whole milk, at room temperature

Rounded cup (240 g) sour cream, at room temperature

¼ cup (60 ml) sunflower oil

1 tbsp (15 ml) vanilla extract

⅔ cup (1⅓ sticks; 150 g) unsalted butter, at room temperature

1¾ cups (350 g) granulated sugar

3 large eggs, at room temperature

4 oz (110 g) confetti sprinkles or jimmies (see Note)

Begin the buttercream: In a small, heavy-bottomed saucepan, whisk together the flour, sugar, salt and milk. Cook over medium to high heat, whisking constantly so the mixture doesn't burn or catch on the bottom of the pan. Once it starts to thicken and you notice bubbling, cook for another 2 minutes, still whisking continuously, until it resembles pastry cream. This whole process could take up to 10 minutes.

When the pudding base is done, strain it through a sieve onto a shallow plate to get rid of any lumps. Cover it with plastic wrap touching the surface to prevent a skin from forming and let it cool to room temperature. You can speed up the process by letting it cool in the fridge, but prior to using, it must be room temperature.

Make the cake: Preheat the oven to 350°F (175°C) or 325°F (160°C) if using a fan-assisted oven. Lightly grease a 9 x 13–inch (23 x 33–cm) baking pan with cooking spray or butter and line with parchment paper that overhangs the two long sides for easier handling later.

Sift 2½ cups (320 g) of the flour, the baking powder and salt into a medium-sized bowl and whisk to combine. In a measuring jug, lightly whisk together the milk, sour cream, sunflower oil and vanilla.

Using a stand mixer fitted with the paddle attachment, beat the butter with half of the sugar until pale and fluffy, 2 to 3 minutes. Add the rest of the sugar and beat to combine. Add the eggs, one at a time, making sure each is fully incorporated before adding the next.

Next, add the flour mixture in three additions, alternating with the sour cream mixture to avoid splashing and overmixing the batter. After each addition, mix the batter just until combined. Scrape the bowl a couple of times with a silicone spatula to make sure everything is mixed nicely.

Mix the sprinkles with 1 tablespoon (8 g) of flour, making sure each sprinkle is coated with flour. Fold the sprinkles into the batter.

(continued)

Sprinkles, for decorating

Scrape the batter into the prepared pan and spread it evenly, then bake for 30 to 35 minutes. It's best to check the cake after 30 minutes and then adjust the baking time accordingly, because ovens can vary. The cake is done when it's springy on the top and when a skewer inserted into the middle comes out mostly clean. Remove it from the oven and leave to cool in the pan on a wire rack for 15 to 20 minutes to firm up a little bit before removing from the pan to cool completely.

While the cake is cooling, finish the buttercream: Using a stand mixer fitted with the paddle attachment, beat the butter for 5 minutes, or until it's pale and fluffy, then add the previously made pudding base, one spoonful at a time. Beat everything until nicely incorporated with no lumps. Add the vanilla and beat for a couple of seconds, or until smooth and combined. Lastly, if desired, add some gel food coloring—a pea-sized amount should do—and beat until fully incorporated and no white streaks are visible.

Transfer the buttercream to a large piping bag fitted with French open star nozzle and pipe dollops on top of the cooled cake. Top with more sprinkles, if desired.

Keep the cake tightly covered in plastic wrap or in an airtight container at room temperature for 2 days or in the fridge for up to a week. Allow it to come to room temperature before serving.

> **Note:** Don't use nonpareils or any other very small or thin type of sprinkles, because they will melt and you won't get the desired colorful look.

Brown Butter Vanilla Loaf Cake

While this is not a classic per se, I look at it as an elevated buttery vanilla pound cake. And oh boy, does it deliver. Brown butter just gives an indulgent dessert the most beautiful nutty aroma and makes the buttery part of the cake stand out even more. I actually ended up eating these leftovers for breakfast, slightly toasted after a couple of days and smeared with some apricot jam on top. And you know what? It was the best. Breakfast. Ever.

. . . .

Serves 10 to 12

Brown Butter
1 cup (2 sticks; 225 g) unsalted butter, sliced

Cake
Cooking spray or butter, for pan

2 cups (250 g) all-purpose flour

2 tsp (10 g) baking powder

½ tsp fine sea salt

Rounded ¾ cup (180 g) sour cream, at room temperature

2 tsp (10 ml) vanilla extract

1¼ cups (250 g) granulated sugar

3 large eggs, at room temperature

Note: For a classic sugar icing, see the directions for the glaze (leaving out the rosewater) of the Raspberry Rose Loaf Cake (page 66).

Brown the butter: In a light-colored skillet, melt the butter over medium-high heat, stirring constantly, until it becomes foamy, then turns clear and starts showing golden brown specks. You'll also notice a nutty aroma. It's done after about 5 minutes, at a medium brown stage. Transfer the butter to a metal bowl and place in the fridge to firm up. Stir it occasionally so it firms up evenly and gets to a room-temperature consistency. Make sure it is at room temperature before using.

Make the cake: Preheat the oven to 350°F (175°C) or 325°F (160°C) if using a fan-assisted oven. Grease a 9 x 5–inch (23 x 13–cm) loaf pan with cooking spray or butter and line with parchment paper over-hanging the two longer sides for easier handling later. If you are using a smaller pan, you'll have some leftover batter, which you can easily bake as cupcakes.

Sift the flour, baking powder and salt into a medium-sized bowl and whisk to combine. In a measuring jug, lightly whisk together the sour cream and vanilla.

In a large bowl, using an electric hand mixer, beat the room-temperature brown butter and sugar on medium-high speed for 2 to 3 minutes, or until it turns pale and fluffy. Add the eggs, one at a time, making sure each is fully combined before adding the next. Scrape the bowl a couple of times with a silicone spatula to make sure everything is mixed nicely.

Next, add the flour mixture to the butter mixture in three additions, alternating with the sour cream mixture. After each addition, beat the mixture just until everything is incorporated to avoid overmixing the batter. Fill the loaf pan about three-quarters of the way full with the cake batter. Using an offset palette knife, smooth out the top.

Bake for 45 to 50 minutes. The cake is done when it's springy on the top and when a skewer inserted into the middle comes out mostly clean. Once the cake is done, remove it from the oven, place it on a wire rack and let it cool in the pan for about 15 minutes before removing from the pan to cool completely.

Keep the cake tightly covered in plastic wrap or in an airtight container at room temperature for 2 days or in the fridge for up to a week. Allow it to come to room temperature before serving.

Red Velvet Cake

Did you know that the original red velvet cake was actually made with ermine frosting and not the cream cheese one? I hope I haven't upset you with this revelation! While I've seen many debates online over whether red velvet falls under the chocolate cake or vanilla cake umbrella, my sister described its flavor as one similar to sweet, just barely chocolate cereal, and I couldn't agree more. It's certainly a unique flavor. It has the best of both worlds: It's red and it's covered in lots of buttercream roses—a guaranteed showstopper whether you consider it a chocolate cake or not!

Serves 12 to 14

Vanilla Buttercream
Scant ½ cup (55 g) all-purpose flour

Rounded cup (225 g) granulated sugar

½ tsp fine sea salt

Scant 1⅔ cups (390 ml) whole milk

1½ cups + 2 tsp (3 sticks + 2 tsp; 350 g) unsalted butter, at room temperature

1 tbsp (15 ml) vanilla extract

Red gel food coloring

Red Velvet Cake
Cooking spray or butter, for pans

Rounded 1¾ cups (230 g) all-purpose flour

3 tbsp (20 g) natural cocoa powder

1½ tsp (7.5 g) baking powder

½ tsp fine sea salt

¼ tsp powdered red food coloring (or more)

1 cup (240 ml) buttermilk, at room temperature (see Notes)

3 tbsp (45 ml) sunflower oil

1 tsp vanilla extract

½ cup (1 stick; 115 g) unsalted butter, at room temperature

1⅓ cups (275 g) granulated sugar

3 large eggs, at room temperature

¼ tsp baking soda

1 tsp white vinegar

Begin the buttercream: In a small, heavy-bottomed saucepan, whisk together the flour, sugar, salt and milk. Cook over medium to high heat, whisking constantly so the mixture doesn't burn or catch on the bottom of the pan. Once it starts to thicken and you notice bubbling, cook for another 2 minutes, still whisking continuously, until it resembles pastry cream. This whole process could take up to 10 minutes.

When the pudding base is done, strain it through a sieve onto a shallow plate to get rid of any lumps. Cover it with plastic wrap touching the surface to prevent a skin from forming and let it cool to room temperature. You can speed up the process by letting it cool in the fridge, but prior to using, it must be room temperature.

Make the cake: Preheat the oven to 350°F (175°C) or 325°F (160°C) if using a fan-assisted oven. Grease three 6-inch (15-cm) round cake pans with cooking spray or butter and line the bottoms with parchment paper.

Sift the flour, cocoa powder, baking powder, salt and powdered red food coloring into a medium-sized bowl and whisk to combine. In a measuring jug, lightly whisk together the buttermilk, sunflower oil and vanilla.

Using a stand mixer fitted with the paddle attachment, beat the butter with half of the sugar until pale and fluffy, 2 to 3 minutes. Add the rest of the sugar and beat to combine. Add the eggs, one at a time, making sure each is fully incorporated before adding the next.

Next, add the flour mixture in three additions, alternating with the sour cream mixture to avoid splashing and overmixing the batter. After each addition, mix the batter just until combined. Scrape the bowl a couple of times with a silicone spatula to make sure everything is mixed nicely. Lastly, mix the baking soda with the vinegar. Once it is done frothing, add it to the batter and gently fold it in using a silicone spatula.

Divide the batter equally by weight among the prepared pans and level it with an offset palette knife, then bake for 22 to 25 minutes. Check the cakes after 22 minutes and then adjust the baking time accordingly. The cakes are done when they're springy on top and a skewer inserted into the middle comes out mostly clean. Remove them from the oven and leave in their pans on a wire rack for 10 to 15 minutes to firm up a bit before removing them from the pans to cool completely.

(continued)

While the cakes are cooling, finish the buttercream: Using a stand mixer fitted with the paddle attachment, beat the butter for 5 minutes, or until it's pale and fluffy, then add the previously made pudding base, one spoonful at a time. Beat everything until nicely incorporated with no lumps. Lastly, add the vanilla and beat for another 15 to 30 seconds, until smooth and combined.

Assemble the cake: Start by leveling the tops of your cakes using a cake leveler or a long, serrated knife for a neater look, if needed. Then, put a little bit of buttercream in the middle of a serving plate or your cake board to keep the cake from moving around. Place it on a turntable for easier handling and decorating.

Place one cake layer on the serving plate and, using a small, offset palette knife or a piping bag filled with buttercream, spread the frosting over the top of the cake layer, about ⅜ inch (1 cm) thick. Top it with the next cake layer and repeat the process. Place the final cake layer on top, making sure it's upside down to get a nice, smooth surface on top.

Next, apply a thin layer of frosting around the cake and smooth it using a cake scraper to keep in the crumbs. Chill the cake in the fridge for 30 to 60 minutes before applying the final coat of frosting.

Divide the remaining frosting among three bowls, leaving one portion slightly larger than the others because that needs to cover the top of the cake. Using red gel food coloring, tint the buttercream in 3 different shades: dark red, light red and rose (use rose for the larger amount of frosting). Put each shade into its own piping bag fitted with an open star nozzle. If you don't have three piping bags, that's okay; it will just take a little longer.

Divide the cake into thirds by marking little lines with an offset palette knife, with the top third being slightly narrower than the bottom and middle one. Start by piping rosettes with the darkest frosting on the bottom third of the cake. Pipe the next row in the light red color, starting in between the two bottom rosettes and overlapping slightly with the row below to avoid any gaps. Continue with the next layer using the rose frosting, and pipe rosettes on top of the cake so the whole cake is covered.

Keep the cake covered at room temperature for 2 days or up to a week in the fridge. Allow it to come to room temperature before serving for the best flavor.

Notes: If you'd like to pair the cake with cream cheese frosting, you can use the one for the Carrot Walnut Sheet Cake (page 147), but keep in mind that you won't be able to make the rosette decorations. Alternatively, use your favorite cream cheese frosting.

If you don't have buttermilk, you can make a substitute by mixing 1 cup (240 ml) of whole milk with 2 tablespoons (30 ml) of fresh lemon juice. Leave it for 10 to 15 minutes, or until it thickens.

German Chocolate Cake

On my quest to learn all about the American classics, I was struggling to figure out what exactly was of German influence in this cake. It turned out I was right, that the "German" in the name actually refers to a baker and chocolate maker who created the recipe, not the country—ha! While the traditional version makes a lighter, milder chocolate cake, I couldn't not use my favorite chocolate cake recipe. The sweet custard-based pecan coconut filling works perfectly against a very rich chocolate cake, creating a decadent dessert worthy of any occasion.

Serves 12 to 14

Chocolate Cake
Cooking spray or butter, for pans

Scant 1½ cups (180 g) all-purpose flour

⅔ cup (75 g) Dutch-processed cocoa powder

2¼ tsp (12 g) baking powder

¾ cup (150 g) granulated sugar

⅔ cup (150 g) soft light brown sugar

½ tsp fine sea salt

Rounded ¾ cup (180 g) sour cream, at room temperature

½ cup (125 ml) sunflower oil

2 large eggs, at room temperature

1 tsp vanilla extract

½ cup + 1 tbsp (135 ml) hot water

Coconut Pecan Filling
2.5 oz (75 g) chopped pecans

2.5 oz (75 g) unsweetened shredded coconut

2 large egg yolks

¾ cup (150 g) granulated sugar

¼ tsp fine sea salt

¾ cup (180 g) evaporated milk

⅓ cup + 1 tsp (⅔ stick + 1 tsp; 80 g) unsalted butter, cubed

Make the cake: Preheat the oven to 350°F (175°C) or 325°F (160°C) if using a fan-assisted oven. Grease three 6-inch (15-cm) round cake pans with cooking spray or butter and line the bottoms with parchment paper.

Sift the flour, cocoa powder, baking powder, granulated and brown sugars and salt into a large bowl and whisk to combine. In a measuring jug, lightly whisk together the sour cream, sunflower oil, eggs and vanilla. Add the sour cream mixture to the flour mixture and whisk to combine into a thick batter. Lastly, add the hot water in two additions and whisk until smooth.

Divide the batter equally by weight among the prepared pans and level it with an offset palette knife. Bake for 23 to 28 minutes. It's best to check the cakes after 23 minutes and then adjust the baking time accordingly, because ovens can vary. The cakes are done if they spring back when lightly touched and when a skewer inserted into the middle comes out mostly clean. Remove them from the oven and leave them to cool in the pans for 10 minutes to firm up before inverting onto a wire rack to cool completely.

Make the coconut pecan filling: In a dry skillet, toast the pecans and coconut over medium-high heat, until golden brown and aromatic, stirring frequently. This should take about 2 to 3 minutes. Set aside until needed.

In a small, heavy-bottomed saucepan, vigorously whisk together the egg yolks, sugar and salt to combine. Pour in the evaporated milk in a slow and steady stream, while whisking constantly, until fully incorporated. Bring the mixture to a simmer over medium-high heat, whisking frequently. Continue to cook, whisking constantly, until the mixture thickens to a pudding consistency. Remove from the heat and stir in the pecans, coconut and butter until smooth and combined. Cover and set aside to cool completely.

(continued)

Dark Chocolate Ganache
3.5 oz (100 g) dark chocolate, at least 55%, finely chopped

6½ tbsp (100 g) heavy cream

Coconut flakes, for sprinkling

Make the dark chocolate ganache: Place the dark chocolate in a medium-sized, heatproof bowl. In a small saucepan, bring the cream to a simmer, then pour it over the chocolate. Cover with a plate and let sit 1 to 2 minutes, or until the chocolate starts to melt. Stir gently with a spatula until creamy, smooth and combined. Cover with plastic wrap and leave to cool and thicken.

Assemble the cake: Start by leveling the tops of your cakes using a cake leveler or a long, serrated knife for a neater look, if needed. Then, put a little bit of ganache in the middle of a serving plate or your cake board to keep the cake from moving around. Place it on a turntable for easier handling and decorating.

Place one cake layer on the serving plate and spread the filling all over. Top it with the next cake layer and repeat the process. Place the final cake layer on top, making sure it's upside down to get a nice, smooth surface on top. Spread the ganache topping over the top of the cake, making rustic swirls with the back of a spoon. Sprinkle some coconut flakes around the top edges for decoration, if desired.

Because of the egg-based filling, keep this cake tightly covered in the fridge for up to a week, but allow it to come to room temperature before serving.

Note: Since the cake is left "naked," it will dry out quicker than other cakes if not stored and covered properly.

Chocolate Vanilla Swiss Roll

A simple flavor in a simple cake for a simple gathering or whenever the sugar craving hits: That's how I see this cake. It comes together in under an hour and the swirl pattern always leaves everyone impressed, so make sure to have this classic recipe under your belt. Both the cake and the filling are extremely light, so the chocolate topping adds a little bit of decadent richness.

Serves 10 to 12

Sponge Cake
Cooking spray or butter, for baking sheet

Rounded ½ cup (70 g) all-purpose flour

Rounded ¼ cup (30 g) Dutch-processed cocoa powder

½ tsp baking powder

¼ tsp fine sea salt

4 large eggs, at room temperature

¾ cup (150 g) granulated sugar

½ tsp vanilla extract

2 tbsp (30 ml) sunflower oil

Powdered sugar, for dusting

Whipped Cream Filling
1 cup + 2 tsp (250 g) heavy cream, cold

¼ cup (30 g) powdered sugar

1½ tsp (8 ml) vanilla extract

Chocolate Glaze
5.5 oz (150 g) dark chocolate, finely chopped

¾ cup + 1 tbsp (200 g) heavy cream

Make the cake: Preheat the oven to 350°F (175°C) or 325°F (160°C) if using a fan-assisted oven. Grease a 10 x 15-inch (25 x 38-cm) baking sheet with cooking spray or butter and line it with parchment paper. Lightly grease the parchment paper, too.

Sift the flour, cocoa powder, baking powder and salt into a medium-sized bowl, whisk to combine and set aside until needed. In the bowl of a stand mixer fitted with the whisk attachment, beat the eggs, granulated sugar and vanilla on medium-high speed for 5 to 8 minutes, or until the mixture becomes pale, doubles in size and falls off the beater in ribbons. Then, add the sunflower oil and mix until well incorporated. Lastly, gradually fold in the flour mixture until everything is combined.

Pour the batter gently onto the prepared baking sheet and spread evenly all the way into the corners using an offset palette knife. Bake for 12 to 15 minutes, or until the cake springs back to the touch. Check after 12 minutes and then adjust the baking time accordingly.

Generously sprinkle a clean kitchen towel with powdered sugar. This prevents the cake from sticking to the towel. When the cake is done baking, remove it from the oven and leave it in the pan for 2 minutes and then flip the cake onto the prepared towel. Carefully peel off the parchment paper and starting at the shorter end, tightly roll the cake up within the towel. It's imperative to do it while still hot, otherwise it will crack later. Leave to cool.

Make the whipped cream filling: In the bowl of a stand mixer fitted with the whisk attachment, combine the cream, powdered sugar and vanilla. Whip on high speed until stiff peaks form, being careful not to overbeat it.

Assemble the cake: Unroll the cooled cake carefully and spread evenly with the filling using an offset palette knife. Roll the cake back up carefully and gently lift it onto a wire rack set over a baking sheet to catch the ganache dripping.

Make the chocolate glaze: Place the dark chocolate in a medium-sized, heatproof bowl. In a small saucepan, bring the cream to a simmer, then pour it over the chocolate. Cover with a plate and let sit for 1 to 2 minutes, or until the chocolate starts to melt. Stir gently with a spatula until creamy, smooth and combined. Pour the ganache all over the cake and refrigerate for at least 30 minutes before serving. The cake is best the same day, but you can keep it in the fridge, tightly covered with plastic wrap to avoid drying for 2 to 3 days.

Acknowledgments

Thank YOU.

To Page Street Publishing, without whom this book wouldn't have been possible. Thank you for giving little ol' ME this wonderful opportunity. It still feels surreal, and I'll forever be grateful.

A special thank-you goes to my editor, Emily Taylor, for always being so kind, helpful and understanding. I couldn't have done it without your support.

To my family, my mom and especially my younger siblings: Thank you for putting up with me and my never-ending panic during the holiday baking, for always being willing to taste test and for giving me honest feedback. I know, I know . . . you deserve some macarons, pies and doughnuts after all these cakes!

To my dad, for always believing in me, especially when I couldn't do it myself. For lifting me up in all the right moments, whenever it was necessary. For giving me a chance to do what I love. For getting me my first camera. Thank you.

To my girls, my harem: Thank you for supporting me from the very beginning—you know, the cringey one. For understanding and not giving up on me in difficult times, when I was more absent than present. It means more to me than you'll ever know.

To Ivan, for loving me when I couldn't love myself. Thank you for always being genuinely amazed at everything I bake, even though I know you were lying sometimes (looking at you, Earl Grey pastry cream). You deserved a savory food feast from me. (Finally!)

To my food blogger friends, some of whom I've never met in person: Thank you for your selfless support, understanding, encouragement and help whenever I needed it.

To all my readers, followers, friends: This would not have happened if it wasn't for you. Thank you for deeming me worthy of your time and choosing my blog and my recipes for some of your most important events. I promise the best is yet to come.

And lastly, thank you to you, dear reader. Thank you for choosing this book, among many others. I hope it brings you joy and helps you make some great memories.

All my love,

Ana

About the Author

Ana Zelić is a self-taught baker, photographer and blogger from Zagreb, Croatia. She started her blog, Ana's Baking Chronicles, a place dedicated to delicious desserts that put flavor first, while in graduate school in 2018. Since then, layer cakes have become her specialty, while she continues to learn everything there is to know about creating incredible baked goods.

You can find Ana's recipes at anasbakingchronicles.com or follow along on Instagram @anasbakingchronicles.

Index